APPROACHES TO RURAL DEVELOPMENT

By

Dr. M. Lakshmi Narasaiah
M.A., Ph.D.
Professor and Head
Department of Economics
Sri Krishnadevaraya University Post-graduate Centre
Kurnool-518002
A. P.

DISCOVERY PUBLISHING HOUSE
NEW DELHI-110002

Reprinted - 2018

First Published - 2003

ISBN: 978-81-7141-634-9

Approaches to Rural Development

Published by:

DISCOVERY PUBLISHING HOUSE PVT. LTD.

4383/4B, Ansari Road, Darya Ganj

New Delhi-110 002 (India)

Phone: +91-11-23279245, 43596064-65

Fax: +91-11-23253475

E-mail: discoverypublishinghouse@gmail.com

sales@discoverypublishinggroup.com

web: www.discoverypublishinggroup.com

Printed at:

Infinity Imaging Systems

Delhi

Contents

Preface

Poverty has become a horrified devil, spreading its moral clouds over the entire world destroying large human resources at every inch. The fomenting question of poverty has been flung on the face of the world. Poverty curtain has descended right across the face of the world dividing materially and philosophically into two different worlds, two separate planets, two unequal humanities—one embarrassingly rich and the other desperately poor. The most formidable challenge of our time now is to lift this poverty curtain out of sight.

The dimensions of poverty are so alarming in India that it has become synonymous to such an extent that they seem to be inseparable. Near empty stomachs; semi-naked bodies, bare feet, bulging bellies, shriveled limps, sunken cheeks, listless eyes, blank faces and pervasive disease and debility are some of its common identification marks. It shows up in varying degrees all over the country.

Poverty can be defined as the inability to attain a minimum standard of living. The simplest method of determining poverty line is to agree upon a certain level of income or consumer expenditure as necessary to meet the minimum needs of life.

According to Eighth Five Year Plan (1992–97) 30 per cent of the population is below poverty line. This demonstrates that even though a large portion of the rural population was working, it was difficult for them to eke out a decent living even at subsistence level. It is true that there has been a considerable decline in the incidence of rural poverty overtime. In terms of absolute numbers of poor, the decline has been much less. While this can be attributed to the demographic factor, the fact remains that after 50 years of planned development about 200 million are still poor in rural India.

Rural development is accounted as a major strategy for economic development in India. Because 70 per cent of the population is in rural areas. Several strategies to improve the living conditions of the rural poor is an integral part of the planning process in India. For anti-poverty programmes, the Government of India launched growth-oriented strategy and target group programme. IRDP comes under target group programmes for the eradication of poverty in the rural-India.

This research area concentrates on the impact of the IRDP in Anantapur district of the State of Andhra Pradesh.

M. LAKSHMI NARASAIAH

1

Introduction

Poverty has now become a challenge to human civilization, as it has been quenching the arduous and vital force and freezing the life-giving stream of humanity. It has become a horrified devil spreading its moral clouds over the entire world destructing wide human resources at every inch. The tormenting question of poverty has been flung on the face of the world. Poverty curtain has descended right across the fact of the world dividing materially and philosophically into two different worlds, two separate planets, two unequal humanities—one embarrassingly rich and the other desperately poor,[1] the most formidable challenge of our time now is to lift this poverty curtain out of sight.

In India, nearly 75 per cent of the people live in rural areas and 46 per cent of them are below the poverty line. They are afflicted by numerous social evils like illiteracy and social backwardness. Today the rural masses comprise landless agricultural labourers, small and marginal farmers and artisans who have either inadequate or bleak opportunities for development.

Rural poverty has assumed distress dimensions in the Indian context with the increase in the magnitude of the rural poor and the worsening of their living conditions in spite of increase in production, widening of the industrial base and the advancement of Science and Technology. It is against this background that the Government, as a custodian of the welfare of the people in a democratic welfare state, has set out with the noble objective of providing social and economic justice to all categories of the people irrespective of their class or creed.

Estimation of Poverty in India

In fact, poverty of the worst kind was seen in the institution of slavery in India. It has been recorded that slavery was a continuous component of the social and economic life of ancient India. Historical records in India prove that a vast majority of Indians were always in poverty and knew no other life than that of want and starvation.

The first economist who attempted to study poverty in India was Dadabhai Naoroji, who stated his views on Indian poverty in his book entitled *'Poverty in India'* in the year 1888. After Dadabhai Naoroji, it was Gandhi who made a serious attempt to fathom the depth of Indian poverty and seriously thought of ways and means to ameliorate the distressing situation. Another important work in this area is of C.N. Vakil[2] who published a book entitled *'Poverty and Planning in the Year 1963'*, and this study found out the reasons for poverty in India. Lack of adequate work for vast majority of the agricultural population during the off-season, the social system which made one person bear the burden of supporting a large family, faulty educational system etc.[3] In the year 1962, the Government of India appointed a study group to make a thorough study of poverty in India and prepare a report on it and the group estimated that a total of 59.4 per cent of Indians were below the poverty line in 1960-61.

Table—1.1 gives the estimates of rural poverty inferred by various researchers, institutions and agencies and Planning Commission in India from 1960-61 onwards. (*See Table on Page 4,5,6*)

B.S. Minhas, a well known economist and Deputy Chairman of Planning Commission during the year 1963-64 held the view that there should be two levels to measure poverty in

India—one for the urban areas and another for the rural areas. He estimated Rs. 240/- per capita annual consumption expenditure at 1960-61 prices as the bare minimum or poverty line for the urban areas and Rs. 160/- per capita annual consumption expenditure at 1960-61 prices as the bare minimum or poverty line for the rural areas. He estimated 46.0 per cent of Indians live below the poverty line.

Pranab Bardhan, another economist, basing his argument on the assumption that the rural prices are generally lower than the urban prices, calculated Rs. 15/- per head per month (Rs. 180/- per head per annum for rural area and Rs. 252/- per head per annum for the urban areas).

Dandekar and Rath,[4] in their well known book on 'Poverty in India,' estimated that in 1960-61, poverty line for the rural areas was at Rs. 15/- per head per month (Rs. 180/- per head per annum) and Rs. 22.5/- per head per month Rs. 270/- per head per annum) for urban areas. Accordingly, it was found that in 1960-61, 33 per cent of villagers and 49 per cent of urban people lived below the poverty line.

It is clearly evident from Table—1.1 that the percentage of rural population below the poverty line was at different levels. While the researchers like Ojha, Vaidyanathan, Ahluwalia and other economists estimated rural poverty between 40 per cent and 50 per cent, the Planning Commission of India estimated 50.7 per cent during the Sixth Plan Period.

The Eighth Five Year Plan (1992-97) redefined the poverty line in view of the increasing in cost of living and fixed the income level of Rs. 11,000 for poverty line. The Seventh Plan reviewing the impact of anti-poverty programmes mentions: *"There is now evidence to suggest that the process of economic growth and the anti-poverty programmes have made a significant dent on the problems of poverty"*. During the Seventh Plan, the planners hoped that the number of poor people would fall from 273 million in 1984-85 to 211 million by 1989-90. In their over enthusiasm, the planners projected that the percentage of people below the poverty line would decline to 10 per cent by 1994-95 and to a

Table—1.1
A Comparative Statement Showing Different Estimates of Rural Poverty in India

Year	*Organisation/ Researcher*	*Estimated number of poor (in million)*	*% of rural population below poverty line*	*Definition of Poverty based on the study*
1	2	3	4	5
1960-61	Dandekar & Rath	135.0	40.0	Rs. 1.80 p.c.c.e at 1960-61 prices yielding a minimum of 2,250 calories per day.
	Ahluwalia*	152.0	42.0	Rs. 189 p.c.c.e, p.a., at 1960-61 prices.
	Vaidyanathan	213.5	59.5	Rs. 240 p.c.c.e., p.a., at 1960-61 prices.
	Ojha	184.2	51.8	Rs. 216 p.c.c.e., p.a. at 1960-61 prices.
1961-62	Ahluwalia	157.0	42.3	Rs. 180 p.c.c.e., p.a., at 1961-62 prices.
1962-63	NIRD	166.0	44.9	The regression equation between NDP from agriculture and Ahluwalia's time series estimates of incidence poverty.
1963-64	E.P.W. do Costa	161.0	34.6	Three types of classification—destitutes, severe destitutes, and the poor—based on minimum per capita expenditure per annum.
	D.S. Minhas	221.0	57.8	Two alternative levels of Rs. 240 and Rs. 2.00 per capita annual consumption expenditure at 1960-61 prices.
	Ahluwalia	189.0	49.1	Above-mentioned criterion.

(Table—1.1 Contd...)

1	2	3	4	5
1964-65	Vaidyanathan	235.7	60.0	As mentioned above (Rs. 240 p.c.c.e., p.a.)
	Bardhan	174.4	51.6	Rs. 180 p.c.c.e., p.a., at 1960-61 prices.
	Ahluwalia	198.0	50.4	Above mentioned criterion.
1965-66	Ahluwalia	205.0	51.1	Above mentioned criterion.
1966-67	Ahluwalia	235.0	57.4	Above mentioned criterion.
1967-68	Ahluwalia	241.0	57.9	Above mentioned criterion.
	Dandekar & Rath	166.4	40.0	Above mentioned criterion.
	Vaidyanathan		67.8	Above mentioned criterion.
	Minhas	210.0	50.6	Rs. 240 p.c.c.e., p.a.,
	Ojha	289.0	70.0	Estimates of minimum desirable income i.e., Rs. 216 to Rs. 480 per annum.
1968-69	Ahluwalia	227.0	53.5	Above mentioned criterion.
1969-70	AFICCI	218.3	41.2	Rs. 240 p.c.c.e., p.a., at 1960-61 prices.
	NIRD	196.0	46.2	Earlier-mentioned criterion.
1970-71	Ahluwalia	217.0	49.1	Earlier-mentioned criterion.
	II PC	198.9	45.0	Rs. 336 p.c.c.e., p.a.,

(Table—1.1 Contd...)

1	2	3	4	5
1971-72	NIRD	183.0	41.5	Earlier mentioned criterion.
1972-73	NIRD	212.0	47.2	Earlier mentioned criterion.
	Planning Commission** (Draft Five Year Plan)	200.00	35.6	Rs. 480 p.c.c.e., p.a., at 1972-73 prices.
1973-74	Ahluwalia	221.0	47.6	Earlier mentioned criterion.
	IIPO	208.0	44.8	Rs. 516 p.c.c.e., p.a.
1974-75	NIRD	232.0	50.1	Earlier mentioned criterion.
1975-76	NIRD	225.0	47.7	Earlier mentioned criterion.
1976-77	NIRD	216.0	45.2	Earlier mentioned criterion.
1977-78	Planning Commission	251.7	50.8	Rs. 741.60 p.c.c.e., p.a, 2,400 calories p.c. per day)
	IIPO	246.4	50.8	Rs. 780 p.c.c.e., p.a., 2,400 calories p.c. per day)
1980-85	Planning Commission	259.6	50.7	Rs. 76 per person per month at current prices (2,400 calories p.c. per day)

* Refers to 1971; ** Refers to 1973; p.c. = per capita; c.e. = consumer expenditure; p.a. = per annum.

Source : G. Morlay Mohan Lal Rural Development and Poverty Alleviation, The Indian Experience, 1986, pp. 12–15.

further level of 5 per cent by 2,000. Although one can dispute with the figures and percentages given, the decline in the number of poor in perceptible as shown by several evaluation studies.

The estimates of poverty reviewed are anything but unanimous. Owing the divergent approaches, norms and methodologies, different economists have arrived at different estimates of the number of poor people in India. There can be an unending debate on the correctness of one estimate or another. Yet, "Judged by any reasonable standards, the extent of abject poverty in rural India is alarmingly massive. The precise estimate of whether it is two-fifths or one-half of rural people, who are beset with crushing poverty today, is a terribly academic matter. A far more important and practical need today is a focus policy analysis on concrete measures for the benefit of the poor, particularly the rural poor, who are more numerous but fail to catch as much attention as the urban poor.[5]

Anti-Poverty Programmes

The Indian planners from the very beginning of the era of planned development have shown their concern for the removal of poverty. The plan documents categorically stated that the benefits of economic development must accrue more and more to the less privileged sections of the society. Various rural development programmes have been implemented to improve the lot of the rural poor.

Growth-oriented Strategy

Till 1970, *'production'* or *'growth'* oriented strategies were followed for improving the living conditions of the poor. The first step for achieving this goal in the context of rural India was the introduction of Community Development Programme (CDP) in 1952 and National Extension Service in 1953. The programme laid emphasis on all-round development of the whole community with special emphasis on weaker and under privileged sections through the use of area development, self help and integrated approaches. The CDP, however, could not bring expected change in the improvement in the conditions of rural masses nor much success could be achieved in the area of agricultural development. This culminated in the adoption of Intensive Agricultural District Programme (IADP) in 1960-61 under which efforts to boost agricultural production were concentrated in areas (16 selected districts) with better prospects of higher yields. The success achieved in increasing agricultural production under this programme led the government to extend it to 117 districts in the country in March, 1964 under the name Intensive Agricultural Area Programme (IAAP). In view of the food crisis emerged in the country as a result of successive droughts during 1964-67. The Government of India launched a new strategy known as High Yielding Varieties Programme (HYVP) in the year 1964-65 which ushered in the so-called *'Green Revolution'*. This has increased the foodgrains production substantially and the country became almost self-sufficient in food by now.

The *'production'* or *'growth'* oriented strategy that was pursued till the end of 1960's did not tackle the problems of poverty and unemployment. The expectations that the process of economic development would transmit the benefit of development widely throughout the society, including the lowest layers did not materialise. Unfortunately, the trickle-down strategy did not work. The gains that accrued from the intensive development efforts, including institutional credit, flowed to the large and resourceful farmers to the neglect of small farmers, agricultural labourers, tenants and rural artisans. Even the technological changes have contributed to the widening of disparities in income between different regions, between small and large farms and between land owners on the one hand and landless labourers on the other.[6] Institutional reforms like Land Ceiling and Land Reform Acts too could not confer benefits on the landless poor.

Target Group Programmes

It was realised that the benefits of various rural development programmes implemented till 1970 were appropriated by those who are better endowed in terms of land resources and the small farmers, agricultural labourers, tenants and other weaker sections, could not derive any advantages. The All India Rural Credit Review Committee set up by the Reserve Bank of India to review the supply of rural credit. Therefore, recommended (1969) for setting up of institutions for the benefit of small and marginal farmers and agricultural labourers. Accordingly, since the start of the Fourth Five Year Plan in 1969, programmes were directed to specific target groups and certain disadvantaged areas. Such programmes included the Small Farmers Development Agency (SFDA), Marginal Farmers and Agricultural Labourers Development Agency (MFALDA), Tribal sub-plan sub-component plans for Scheduled Castes, Antyodaya Scheme and Area Development Programmes like the Drought Prone Area Programme (DPAP), Desert Development Programme (DDP), Hill Area Development Programme (HADP) etc. The Fifth Plan introduced the 20 point economic programme and the Minimum Needs Programme. Thus, the strategy of development during 1970s consisted of target group-oriented programmes and area development programmes which are described briefly hereunder. The guidelines for the implementation of these beneficiary-oriented schemes explicitly prescribe certain coverage for SCs and STs. Specific plans like *'Tribal sub-plan'* for STs and *'Special Component Plan'* for SCs have also been evolved into the regular five year plans.

SFDA and MFALDA

The Small Farmers Development Agency (SFDA) and the Marginal Farmers and Agricultural Labourers Development Agency (MFALDA) which were started in 1971 following the recommendations of the All India Rural Credit Review Committee (1969) were merged into a single agency in 1974. The objective of the programme was to assist persons specially and identified from this target group in raising their income levels. This was to be achieved by helping them, one the one hand, to adopt improved agricultural technology and acquiring means of increasing agricultural production and on the other hand, to diversify farm economy through subsidiary activities like Animal husbandry, Dairying, Horticulture etc. The agencies provide a subsidy of 25 per cent to small farmers and 331/3 per cent to marginal farmers and agricultural labourers on specified capital investments and inputs. The agencies were to make special effort to ensure that the needed inputs and credit were made available to the beneficiaries by respective credit institutions.

Upto March, 1980, the agencies had identified 16.7 million beneficiaries of whom 8 million were assisted. Of those assisted, 6.1 million on 75 per cent were helped to acquire access to improved agricultural practices, through subsidy, supply of inputs and implements and field demonstrations. The remaining 1.9 million beneficiaries were helped to acquire assets like milch cattle, sheep, poultry etc., minor irrigation facilities and village industries units. Among the beneficiaries 1.3 million credit advances to beneficiaries through co-operatives over the years till March, 1980 amounted to Rs. 112.82 crores and Rs. 140.20 crores respectively. The short-term loan from co-operatives and commercial banks were Rs. 27.76 crores and Rs. 6.03 crores respectively in 1979-80. The Government expenditure in the form of subsidy given to beneficiaries and on some other items was Rs. 156.10 crores during 1974-75.

The Sixth Five Year Plan (1980-85) notes that only half of the beneficiaries were assisted and the bulk of the assistance did not lead to asset creation. The principle reason for a lower coverage under such asset creation purposes has been the progressive erosion in the integrated functioning of the block agency which is the main implementation agency, inadequacies of the credit institutions and lack of co-ordination and adequate support from concerned departments to the agencies programmes.[7] It was also found that in several cases some of the big landlords transferred their land in the names of their sons, etc., and got them identified as small farmers.[8] In the year 1980-81, SFDA was merged with IRDP.

Realising that unemployment and under-employment are the important causes for rural poverty, the Government of India started implementing income generating employment schemes for the rural poor. These programmes are:

Crash Scheme for Rural Employment (CSRE)

The Crash Scheme for Rural Employment was introduced as non-plan programme with effect from 1971-72 and it was upgraded as a Central Plan programme in the next year. The selected rural works under CSRE should be located in areas of each district where other special programmes such as SFDA are not in operation; where the percentage of landless labour and the incidence of unemployment is relatively high and those which are relatively less developed. The basic objective of the CSRE is to generate employment in productive works for a 1,000 persons in each district, on an average 2.50 lakh man-days of employment should be generated in every district.[9]

One striking defect of CSRE is that overstressed the importance of job creation and neglected the more important objective of creation of appropriate assets. Huge amounts were incurred particularly to fulfil the financial targets. Manpower can be utilised on a wide variety of schemes. Minor irrigation, soil conservation, flood protection, construction of schools, etc. However, 70 to 80 per cent of the expenditure was on the so-called road building. The district administration in charge of the amounts allotted to the scheme was not prepared to provide suitable organisational machinery to formulate, select and execute such projects which strengthen the productive assets. While allotting funds for various blocks, the regional variation in development were not taken into account. There was undue delay in the selection and implementation of schemes.[10]

Food for Work Programme (FFW)

This programme was introduced by the Government of India in 1977-78 as a non-plan scheme to augment the funds of the state governments for the maintenance of public works. It aimed at creation of additional employment in rural areas for building up of durable community assets (such as irrigation tanks, school buildings, panchayat buildings, drinking water well, laying of village streets, drainage etc., with the use of surplus foodgrains available for part payment of wages. In the beginning somewhat hesitantly the programme gained momentum in 1978-79 when over 12 lakh tonnes of foodgrains were utilised creating 372.8 million man-days employment. During the year 1979-80, 23 lakh tonnes of foodgrains were allotted resulting in about 600 to 700 million man-days employment. The programme, besides creating substantial additional employment in rural areas during the lien periods, more particularly in areas affected by drought in 1979, made a favourable impact in the stabilisation of wages and also helped to check foodgrain prices in rural areas. An evaluation of the programme by the Planning Commission revealed that in the 10 states studied, 50.6 per cent of the sample beneficiaries were agricultural labourers, 22.4 per cent were cultivators, 19.7 per cent were non-agricultural labourers and 17.3 per cent were others.[11] Although the programme was quite successful in generating employment, it suffered from limitations. Since it was implemented on year to year basis, the state government felt uncertainty about its continuance and hence did not create an administrative machinery for its effective implementation. This programme was merged in the National Rural Development Programme in 1980.

Minimum Needs Programme (MNP)

The concept of MNP emerged and crystallised out of the previous experience of plans that neither growth nor social consumption can be sustained, much less accelerated, without being mutually supportive.[12] The MNP was first introduced in 1974-75 with the objective of establishing a network of basic services and facilities of social consumption designed to assist in raising consumption levels of those living below the poverty line and thereby improve the productive efficiency of the people, the basic needs of the people identified for this programme include elementary education, adult education, rural health, rural roads, rural water supply, rural housing, rural electrification and nutrition. In respect of the urban areas, the programme aims at the development of urban slums.

The implementation of the MNP for a decade between 1974-75 and 1984-85 provided certain lessons on the basis of which the major thrust of the programme during the Seventh Plan (1985-90) was oriented towards integration of the MNP with other rural development and anti-poverty programmes. The basic logic in establishing this linkage can be explained as follows: The MNP comprises two distinct sets of activities. The first is human resource development activities such as elementary and adult education, health, drinking water supply, rural housing and nutrition. The second relates to area development activities such as rural roads and village electrification, thc various components of MNP, thus seek to enhance and productive capacity of the community as a whole.[13]

Antyodaya Programme

Antyodaya, a Gandhian concept, is another strategy of developing the rural poor. Rajasthan was the first state to introduce this programme on October, 2, 1977. Later on, it was adopted in other states also. Antyodaya, as the name implies, is the upliftment of the *'last man in the row'*.

It aims at raising the living standards of the poorest of the poor in the villages. This will be a great help to them in making them self-reliant and enabling them to take advantage of the general development programmes.[14] There are basically four salient features of the Antyodaya programme. Firstly, poverty does not remain, merely a statistical abstraction. The poor family is realised as a concrete human reality. Secondly, stress is to be laid on the delivery of production assets so that the poor family begins to get regular income from self-employment. Thirdly, the government officials themselves proceed to villages to identify the poorest among the poor instead of waiting for people to come for assistance. Fourthly, the parameters adopted for selecting families for this programme is strictly followed on the economic basis (income below the poverty line) which varies from state to state.[15]

Being the basic unit of implementation at the field level the block administration has been charged with the responsibility for proper identification of the beneficiaries and also for the implementation and supervision of Antyodaya programme. In otherwords, it also means that this programme is to live with all kinds of deficiencies and defects in the functioning of the blocks.[16] An important recommendation made by the programme evaluation organisation of the Planning Commission is that there is an urgent need to have a well-defined machinery for implementing the programme of Antyodaya as also its follow up.

Area Development Programme

Although some target group oriented programmes are introduced for the benefit of the rural poor, it was realised that in certain areas the mere implementation of such programmes would not solve the problem of abject poverty. There are backward areas like drought prone areas, desert areas, tribal areas, etc., which require special efforts for their development. The Area Development Programme that have been introduced are as follows.

Drought Prone Area Programme (DPAP)

There were certain areas in the country which could not develop owing to the scarcity of rainfall. Nearly one-fifth of India's total land area suffers from varying degrees of scarcity in rainfall and is thus subject to drought.[17] In 1970, the Government of India launched the Rural Works Programme (RWP) in these areas as an employment-oriented programme with special emphasis on labour-intensive employment opportunities in soil conservation, afforestation, road construction, and provision of irrigation facilities. However, the RWP was unable to provide employment avenues on a regular basis. In 1972-73, the RWP was modified and given the name of the drought prone area programme. The DPAP was originally designed as an employment generation programme but later on its focus shifted to development works so that it could provide a permanent solution to the problems of drought rather than piecemeal solutions to the problem of unemployment. The sole responsibility of administering the DPAP rests with the District Rural Development Agency (DRDA).

The aim of the programme was conservation, development and utilisation in an optimum manner of land, water, live-stock and human resources in the selected districts the main thrust of efforts is in the direction of restoration of a proper ecological balance in the above district. For this the concept of integrated area development was linked to watershed approach. But the officials considered DPAP a source of additional funds and no attempt was made for an integrated watershed development. Thus, no progress or improvement could be seen in restoring ecological balance. The programme is under implementation in 615 blocks spread over 91 districts in 13 states.[18]

During 1974-75, 1979-80, the total allocation for this programme was Rs. 384 crores and out of this Rs. 328.66 were actually spent.[19] The Sixth Plan allocation for DPAP was Rs. 350 crores. As against this, the actual expenditure amounted to Rs. 310 crores. The Seventh Plan allocations for this programme was Rs. 462.76 crores. As against this, the actual expenditure was Rs. 459.45 crores. The creation of irrigation potential during the plan period was 2,23,585 thousand hectares,[20] unfortunately, as per a number of studies, the fruits of DPAP assistance have been by and large, concerned by minority of big farmers and availed by better endowed areas, as they easily adopt the modern agricultural practices, conversely the small and marginal farmers who are capital deficient and generally illiterate, adopt it at later stage because of demonstration effect. Apparently, the least sufferers from drought have been the landlords and money-lenders-cum-traders. This minority easily corners huge capital by selling the accumulated inventory of foodgrains in the market.

Integrated Tribal Development Agency (ITDA)

After the advent of Independence, the Government of India formulated several policies and programmes and established institutions to develop the tribal areas. The Renuka Ray Report of 1959 pointedly referred to the need for an integrated approach to tribal development. The Scheduled Caste and Scheduled Tribes Commission under the Chairmanship of Debar in 1960 stressed an integrated approach and believed that, *"the problem of economic development for the bulk of the tribals cannot be solved unless the resources of land, forest, cattle wealth, cottage and village industries are all mobilised in an integrated way"*. The S.C. Dube Commission in 1972 which was set up to advise on tribal development in the Fifth Plan was of the belief that time bound Integrated Area Development Programme could no longer be postponed because it was absolutely urgent. With the intention of promoting the tribal areas in a more integrated way. An Integrated Tribal Development Programme (ITDP) was launched in 1974 during the Fifth Five Year Plan period (1974-79). The states were asked the frame tribal sub-plans for areas of tribal concentration. The blocks where more than 50 per cent of the population comprised tribals were to be included in the tribal sub-plan for the implementation of ITDP. It was hoped that with the introduction of ITDP more resources would flow into the tribal areas for tribal development. The basic objectives of the sub-plan and ITDA are to narrow down the gap between the backwardness of tribal areas and the economically and socially developed areas, with a view to improve the quality of life of these long depressed people.[21] Further elimination of exploitation in all forms, speeding up the process of socio-economic development and improving their organisational capacity, are the major objectives of the Agency.[22]

The funding of tribal sub-plans has been going up very substantially in recent years. In the fifth plan period, the amount was Rs. 1,182 crores. In the next plan period, it rose by almost 5 times to Rs. 5,500 crores. In the Seventh Plan period it has again risen, being almost double of the previous one (i.e. Rs. 10,500 crores.) Not only the flows from the state outlays have increased very substantially and grants from sectorial union ministers for specific programmes have gone up but also central special assistance and institutional credit have risen significantly.[23]

For the operational purpose the tribal sub-plan areas have organised 178 Integrated Tribal Development Projects during the Fifth Five Year Plan. It is at this level the entire development efforts have been integrated. By the end of the Fourth Year of the Sixth Five Year Plan, 181 of ITDPs were in operation in the country. The coverage of state population during the plan rose to about 75 per cent of the total tribal population in the country from about 65 per cent during the fifth five year plan. At the end of the seventh plan, the tribal sub-plan strategy was being implemented through 191 integrated tribal development projects. So far the tribal population covered by ITDP areas is 313.21 lakhs.[24]

Hill Area Development Programme

The Hill areas of the country, particularly the Himalayan and the Western Ghats regions which constitute about 21 per cent of the total area and contain 9 per cent of the total population of the country, support the basic live-giving natural resources but have fragile and sensitive eco-systems. The need to conserve natural resources and the environment particularly to prevent damage to fragile and irreplaceable eco-systems, has been voiced in national policies and programmes for quite some time. The Hill Area Development Programme was started in 1972-73, has been a major step in this regard. The programme emphasized the partial utilisation of the resources of the hill areas through the specially designed programmes for the development of horticulture, plantations, agriculture, animal husbandry, forestry, soil conservation and suitable village industries. The focus is essentially on a package of activities that could be absorbed by the people inhabiting hilly tracts. Similarly there are schemes for tribal areas, less developed plain areas, where special programmes have been taken up with assistance provided by the Central Government such areas can be categorised either under special area programme, specific target group programme or regional development programme.

Apart from the normal flow of funds to the hill areas from the state plans, in consideration of the regional imbalance and other special factors, special central assistance (SCA) is being provided for the HADP. An allocation of Rs. 170 crores, inclusive of Rs. 20 crores for Western Ghats Development Programme

(WGDP) was made for the fifth plan. It was raised to Rs. 560 crores (including Rs. 75 crores for WGDP) in the Sixth Plan. The Seventh Plan allocation of SCA is Rs. 870 crores, inclusive of Rs. 116.50 crores for WGDP. The pattern of assistance comprises 90 per cent grant and 10 per cent loan. In so far as category (a) of the designed hill areas is concerned, the available SCA is allocated among the constituent states, giving equal weightage to area and population. In the case of areas in category (b) excluding the Nilgiris district (which is covered by the former category), the weightage for area is 75 per cent and for population 25 per cent. In order to ensure, integration and linkages of schemes formulated under SCA with other sources of funding like the state plans, a sub-plan approach has been adopted. But in the case of WGDP, a scheme-wise approach has been followed.[25]

The programme was titled in favour of beneficiary-oriented schemes during the Fifth Plan period. In the Sixth Plan period, eco-development was emphasized, but the general tenor of the plan did not differ significantly from the normal state plan. In other words, they have been characterised by the sectoral approach with adequate reference to eco-restoration, eco-preservation and eco-development.

Command Area Development Programme (CADP)

With the large public sector investment of about Rs. 2,500 crores in major and medium irrigation projects, the need was felt for the optimum utilisation of the irrigation potential. A number of committees and commissions have expressed grave concern about the under-utilisation of irrigation potential created by heavy investments in the past on the other hand, irrigation whenever available did not yield the desired results. For instance, as against potential of 4 to 5 tonnes of foodgrains per hectare, the actual yield was around 1.7 tonnes only. The principal reasons for this shortfall were: (a) inadequate irrigation or over-irrigation due to absence of proper distribution system (b) heavy water-logging conditions in the absence of proper drainage systems leading to increase in water level in the

Command Areas and soil salinity in large areas (c) some areas included in the cultivable command areas not getting water for irrigation and (d) inadequate use of strategic agricultural inputs in the absence of proper water control structures. It was therefore, felt that an integrated area development approach should be adopted in dealing with all these points in order to ensure optimum production. This matter came up for consideration before the irrigation commission and was also dealt with by the National Commission on Agriculture.

Based on the recommendations of the Irrigation Commission and the National Commission on Agriculture, the Command Area Development Programme was introduced (1974-75) during the Fifth Five Year Plan as a centrally sponsored scheme. The principal objective of the programme was to increase the utilisation of the irrigation potential below the outlet command thereby increasing productivity per unit of land and water. This was to be achieved through an integrated system of effective water distribution and efficient soil-crop-water management practices. By the end of March, 1990 an area of about 4.96 million hectares were under warabandi, land levelling and shaping had been done on 1.92 million hectares and field channels is constructed for 11.1 million hectares.[26]

The CAD programme undoubtedly contributed substantially to increase productivity in certain crops throughout the country. For instance, according to one of the studies conducted, increase in kharif paddy per hectare varied from 24.60 quintals in Nagarjunasagar (left bank) to 2 quintals in Kadana command (Gujarat). On the average, the increase has been about 8 quintals per hectare which can be considered as a substantial increase. However, it has not so far been possible for the beneficiaries to derive optimum advantage from such facilities on account of various problems such as non-availability of assured and regular supplies of water in certain irrigation systems, non-construction of field channels, slow progress in land development schemes, the inadequacy of infrastructure and inputs and also inadequate appreciation of the quantum of water required for each of the crops.[27] Thus, this too has been an addition in fragmented and compartmentalised approach to rural development on the part of the Government of India.

Desert Development Programme (DDP)

A subsidiary to the DPAP was the Desert Development Programme launched in 1977-78 in pursuance of the recommendations of the National Commission on Agriculture.[28] Desert areas in the country reflect more acute form of ecological degradation marked by extreme aridity, shifting sand, scanty vegetation, severe wind erosion, etc. The DDP is designed to control the process of desertification and restoration of ecological balance so as to improve the living conditions of the people of these areas. Sand-dune stabilisation, shelter-belt plantation, conservation of surface water and recharge of ground water aquifers, efficient water resources management, afforestation grassland and pasture development and horticulture constitute the activities under this programme. DDP covers 131 blocks of 21 districts in 5 states.[29]

In the first few years the total cost of the programme was borne by the Union Government. During the Sixth Plan period (1980-85) it was shared equally between the Union Government and the state governments concerned. The total allocation made to all the five states was above Rs. 95 crores. The Union Government's contribution was to be Rs. 43 crores. Actually, however the total expenditure was about Rs. 73.5 crores.

Allocation of funds also depends on the severity of arid conditions and Rs. 24 lakhs per 1,000 sq. km. subject to a district ceiling of Rs. 500 lakhs have been allocated for not desert districts. For cold desert district areas, a lumpsum provision is made at the rate of Rs. 100 lakhs per district per year for Himachal Pradesh and Rs. 150 lakhs per district for Jammu and Kashmir. The implementation processes in the DPAP/DDP were weak and faulty. Many schemes were dropped even after they had been sanctioned. The projects started, unnecessarily extended their periods of gestation and mid-term revisions of schemes led to an unavoidable waste of funds.

In the Seventh Plan period the allocation for DDP was Rs. 192.30 crores. Against this the actual expenditure amounted to Rs. 194.04 crores. The irrigation potential created was 232.3 thousand hectares.[30] To ensure participation of the people in planning and implementation of the programmes various measures have been suggested such as preparation of water shed development plan with the help of the people in the watershed itself under the guidance of technical experts and adequate local representation in the watershed development committee was set up for the implementation of the project under these programmes.

Strategy for District Attack on Poverty

By and large, all the programmes (mentioned above) and their approaches were selective, sporadic, piecemeal or sectoral in nature. None of these programmes covered the whole country though a large number of blocks in the country had more than one of these programmes operating simultaneously in the same area for the same target group. This territorial overlap combined with different funding agencies not only created considerable difficulties in monitoring and accounting, it often blurred the programme objectives. In practice these programmes were reduced to mere subsidy giving programme shown of any planned approach to the development of rural poor as an inbuilt process in the development of the area and its resources.

The Sixth Five Year Plan (1980-85) therefore, proposed that *"such a multiplicity of programmes operated by a multiplicity of agencies should be ended and replaced by one single programme operative throughout the country"*. Thus there is a shift in the strategy from indirect to direct programmes for poverty eradication from the Sixth Plan. Poverty alleviation programme became an integral part of the planning process in the Sixth Plan. The goal of poverty alleviation was sought to be achieved through two main instruments: (i) a set of self-employment schemes for the rural poor, i.e., IRDP and its two sub-programmes (a) Training for Rural Youth for Self Employment (TRYSEM-1979) and (b) Development of Women and Children in Rural Areas (DWCRA) launched in 1982-83; and (ii) Wage employment programmes like National Rural Employment Programme (NREP—1980) and Rural Landless Employment Guarantee Programme (RLEGP—1982). These have now been merged into Jawahar Rozgar Yojana (JRY) in 1989.

While the first set of programme aim at giving the poor family an income generating asset, the second set provides direct income to the poor through wage employment. The Indira Awas Yojana was also included in the programme in the Seventh Plan for construction of houses for SC/ST and bonded labour. The two supportive programmes of IRDP and the Wage Employment Programme are discussed in Chapter 2 in detail.

Integrated Rural Development Programme (IRDP)

The programme was launched in the year 1976-77 on a pilot basis with an adhoc budgetary provision of Rs. 15 crores in 20 selected districts representing different socio-economic and ecological conditions so that the experience gained in these district could be used in other parts of the country. Later on in 1978-79 IRDP was initiated in 2,300 development blocks. From October 2, 1980, the programme was extended to all the 5,011 development blocks in the country.

The main objective of the IRDP is to make a multi-pronged attack on the problems of rural development with particular emphasis on the removal of poverty and unemployment in rural areas through the adoption of a *'family'* as a unit of development process. In a vast country like India, there are found to be regional variations in resource endowment, levels of development, incidence of poverty. Each region or each district tends to have peculiar problems of its own. Hence micro level studies not only provide greater insights on various aspects relating to the impact of the programme but also point out operational changes that are necessary in block level planning on the basis of the results of such studies.

REFERENCES

1. Haq Mahbudul, *The Poverty Curtain, Choice for the Third World*, Oxford University Press, New Delhi, 1983, Preface XV.

2. C.N. Vakil, *Poverty and Planning,* Allied Publishers, New Delhi, 1963, p. 46.

3. *Ibid.* p. 82.

4. V.M. Dandekar and N. Rath, *'Poverty in India,'.* Allied Publishers, New Delhi, 1970, p. 12.

5. Minhas, B.S., *"Rural Poverty, Numbers, Games and Polimics"*, Indian Economic Review, New series, April, 1971, p. 102.

6. Hanumantha Rao, C.H., *Technological Change and Distribution of Grains in Indian Agriculture,* Mac Millan, Delhi, 1975, p. 178.

7. Planning Commission (17), *Op. cit.*, p. 168.

8. Government of India, Report on *Evaluation Study of Small Farmers, Marginal Farmers and Agricultural Labourers Project, 1974-75,* New Delhi, 1979, p. 5.

9. Sundaram, I.S., *Anti-poverty Rural Development in India,* D.K. Publications, New Delhi, 1984, pp. 181-182.

10. *Ibid.*, p. 183.

11. Planning Commission, *Sixth Five Year Plan (1978-83), Revised Draft, Government of India,* Paras 21.9 and 21.10, p: 304.

12. Sixth Five Year Plan (17), *Op. cit.*, p. 222.

13. Sukhamoy Chakravarthy, *"Development Strategies for Growth with Equity: The South Asian Experience"*, Asian Development Review, Vol. 8, No. 1, 1990, pp. 146-147.

14. *The Supplementary Report of the Comptroller and Auditor General of India for the year 1973-74 (Part-I),* Comptroller and Auditor General of India, New Delhi.

15. Krishna, Raj, *'Antyodaya'*, Yojana, Vol. XXIII, Nos. 14-15, March, 1980, p. 19.

16. Joshi, N.C., *"Antyodaya as it works,"* Kurukshetra, October 1, 1979, p. 45.

17. Maheswari, S., *Rural Development in India*, SAGE Publications, New Delhi, 1985, p. 97.

18. *Government of India, Annual Report* (1990-91), Department of Rural Development, Ministry of Agriculture, New Delhi, p. 51.

19. *Government of India, Annual Report* (1985-86), Department of Rural Development, Ministry of Agriculture, New Delhi, p. 36.

20. *Government of India, Basic Rural Statistics,* Department of Rural Development, Ministry of Agriculture, New Delhi, 1991, p. 37.

21. Harsad, R. Trivedi, "*Salient Features of Tribal Administration in the states,*" Indian Journal of Public Administration, Vol. XXII, No. 3, 1976, p. 515.

22. Sharma, B.D., "*Administration for Tribal Development*", Indian Journal of Public Administration, Vol. XXIII, No. 3, 1977, p. 515.

23. Khanna, B.S., *Rural Development in South Asia-India*, Deep and Deep Publications, New Delhi, 1991, p. 175.

24. Mahalingam, S., *Planned Approach for Tribal Development in India—An appraisal, Administrative and Developmental Perspectives in Tribal Landscapes*, Arihant Publishers, Jaipur, 1992, p. 114.

25. *Planning Commission, Seventh Five Year Plan (1985-90), Vol. II,* Government of India, New Delhi, p. 338.

26. *Planning Commission* (19), p. 60.

27. Tripathy, R.N., "*Command Area Development*", Kurukshetra, August 16, 1980, p. 27.

28. For details, see *the report of the National Commission on Agriculture,* Government of India, 1976.

29. Government of India (33) *Op. cit.*, p. 51.

30. Government of India (35), *Op. cit.* p. 52.

Integrated Rural Development Programme in India

Poverty in Rural Asia remains the most formidable challenge to development. Though economic growth was regarded as the principal instrument of reducing and eliminating poverty, rural poverty increased in South Asian Countries. Trickle Down Theory has not been found to work in large areas of rural Asia. Due to high unequal distribution of land and other assets, large number of households dependent on agricultural labour as the major source of income. Governments in the region had launched different programmes like land to the landless, consolidation of holdings and rural employment generation schemes. But with a few exceptions, rural poverty tended to increase during the sixties and the first half of the seventies. The burden of poverty is spread unevenly among the countries of the developing world and among the regions within the countries. Nearly half of the world's poor live in South Asia, a region that accounts for roughly 30 per cent of the world's population. The poor are often concentrated in certain places in rural areas with high population densities.[1]

It is also realised that *"a mere project approach or a sectoral approach is not adequate to lead to an overall development of the area and distribution of benefits to the local population, particularly the weaker sections of the society. The distribution of unemployment and poverty and the potential for development vary from region to region and also within the region. The efforts will now be to make the programmes area specific and utilise the local endowments for growth for social justice"*.[2] It is therefore considered necessary to plan the integration of various rural development programmes so as to achieve growth with social justice.

Need for Rural Development

Rural development is advocated as a basic strategy for economic development in India. Often, rural development has meant the extension of irrigation, expansion of electricity supply, improvements in the techniques of cultivation, construction of school buildings and the provision of educational facilities, provision of health etc. This is a very narrow view of understanding rural development. Development does not mean simply physical building activities, installation of machines, or adoption of technology. Indeed all this will not serve any purpose if the people inhabiting rural areas are handicapped in utilising these means of development.[3] Rural development is broadly referred to the improvement in the living standards of the low income groups in rural areas and making the process of their development self-sustaining.[4] This implies reducing poverty and human misery by increasing the productivity of the poor and providing them with greater access to goods and services.

Genesis and Evolution of IRDP

The concept of Integrated Rural Development emerged at the annual conference of the Indian Science Congress held at Waltair in January 1976. In March 1976, the Union Finance Minister presented a special paper on *'Strategy of Integrated Rural Development'* which gave details of a rural development programmes directed towards making optimum use of available resources through purposive use of inputs of science and technology for the benefit of rural people. Later on a working group consisting of the representatives of the departments of Rural Development, Agricultural Research and Education (DARE), Science and Technology (DST), the Planning Commission and the Council of Scientific and Industrial Research (CSIR) was set up in May 1976 to suggest norms and to select one district in each state for taking up Integrated Rural Development Projects. Following the criteria suggested by the group, the IRDP was initiated in the year 1976-77 on a pilot basis with an adhoc budget provision of Rs. 15 crores in 20 selected districts representing different socio-economic and ecological conditions so that the experience gained in these districts could be used in other parts of the country. Later on, in 1978-79 the programme was extended to 2,300 development blocks in the country. Out of these, 2,000 blocks were already covered by SFDA, MFALDA, DPAP, CADP etc. It was decided that every year the programme was to be extended to 300 blocks. On October 2, 1980, it was extended to cover all the 5,011 blocks in the country. It is being implemented through a single agency known as District Rural Development Agency (DRDA) at the district level. Upto 1978-79 IRDP was a central sector scheme and 100 per cent funds were provided by the Central Government. Since 1979-80, this programme was made a centrally sponsored scheme in which funding is to be shared on 50:50 basis between the Centre and the States. In the case of Union Territories, however, 100 per cent funds are to be provided by the Centre. The underlying idea of integrated development is that the development package should contain co-ordinated programmes in different sectors which are appropriately linked and spaced out. It involves several categories of integration, i.e.,[5]

(i) integration of sectoral programmes: agriculture, off-farm activities, industry, etc., with forward and backward linkages;

(ii) spatial integration, i.e., integration betw[illegible] areas;

(iii) integration of economic development with social development;

(iv) integration of total area of approach with target group approach;

(v) integration of human resources development with manpower needs by deviating education and training programmes;

(vi) integration of income generating schemes with minimum needs programme of education, rural health, water supply and nutrition; and

(vii) integration of credit with technical services.

Objectives

The IRDP has been conceived as essentially an anti-poverty programme. The basic object was to promote self-employment of the poor households so that with the transfer of productive assets, they may earn incomes that help them to cross the poverty line. The main objectives of IRDP are as follows:

1. increasing production and productivity in agriculture and allied sectors based on better use of land, water and sunlight;
2. creation of new productive assets for improving the lot of the rural people;
3. developing the resource and income of the vulnerable sections of the population in all the blocks of the country;
4. improving the productivity of land by providing access to inputs like water, improved seeds and fertilizers, to those categories of the rural poor, who have some land assets;
5. diversification of agriculture through animal husbandry, dairying, forestry, fishery and sericulture, which will benefit both the landless and the landholders;
6. developing, processing and manufacturing activities based on local resources; and

7. improving post-harvest technology so that both producers and consumers benefit from the enhanced production.

Approach

The approach of IRDP represents the synthesis of (i) cluster approach, (ii) antyodaya approach and (iii) package approach which were tried and found successful in earlier rural development programmes in India. The cluster approach which is based on India's experience with the development programmes such as DADP and CAD is employed for the selection of a cluster of villages for the implementation of the programme. The antyodaya approach which is based on Rajasthan's experience is used for selecting the poorest of the poor for assistance. The package approach requires that each identified and selected beneficiary family is provided with a complete package of necessary inputs, raw materials and services.

Target Group

The target group comprises small and marginal farmers, agricultural and non-agricultural labourers, rural craftsmen and artisans, SCs and STs and in fact all such families of five persons with an annual income of Rs. 3,500. The programme takes *'family'* and not *'individual'* as a unit for development purposes. In order to ensure that the poorest of the poor families get the assistance first families with an annual income level upto Rs. 3,500 are to be associated on priority basis in each Gram Panchayat.

The Seventh Five Year Plan (1985-90) revised the poverty line to Rs. 6,400 per annum for family and the cut off line for identification of families at Rs. 4,800 with the stipulation that all families below Rs. 3,500 income will be taken up first so as to keep the focus on the poorest of the poor.

Out of the assisted families, at least 30 per cent (Sixth Plan) should belong to Scheduled Castes/Tribes. It revised to 50 per cent from April 1, 1990. To ensure better participation of women in the development process, the coverage of women beneficiaries has been increased to 30 per cent in August 1985, from 20 per cent fixed for the first time in June 1985. It was further decided to increase it to 40 per cent from April 1, 1990 onwards. At least 3 per cent of the beneficiaries assisted should be from the category of physically handicapped persons.

Identification of Beneficiaries

The identification of the eligible families out of the target group requires a detailed household survey to assess the income. Therefore, a household survey for this purpose has to be carried out. The surveyed families would then be classified into three income groups, i.e., (i) upto Rs. 2,250 (ii) Rs. 2,251 to Rs. 3,500 and (iii) Rs. 3,501 to Rs. 4,800.

The procedure adopted for the selection of families is as follows:

(i) the list of the poorest of the poor families is prepared by Village Level Worker/Block Staff;

(ii) the list so prepared is then placed for approval in the Village Assembly (Gram Sabha) attended by the block officers, bank officers, non-officials, local people etc. Prominent voluntary action groups are also expected to be associated with these meetings. This meeting is convened by the Block Development Officer concerned;

(iii) the list of the beneficiaries so selected is then displayed on the notice board of the Village Panchayat and the block office.

The forum of Village Assembly is utilised to explain the benefits of different schemes so that beneficiaries can be motivated to adopt a suitable scheme depending upon their ability and experience.

Formulation of Household Plans

For each selected beneficiary, a detailed household plan is to be formulated by the VLW as per the instructions of the

Government of India. The plan format provides for inclusion of such details of each of the schemes proposed to be executed by the household as estimated cost, subsidy and loan to be provided, loan repayment period, amount of loan instalment and estimated net income over a period of time.

Selection of Cluster Villages

Under the operational guidelines for the implementation of IRDP, it laid down that a cluster approach should be adopted. The cluster approach requires, inter alia, the existence, in the villages to be selected, of programme specific supporting infrastructure including credit institutions. The following are the criteria for selection of village clusters, viz., (i) Existence of programme-specific infrastructure, (ii) Availability of credit institutions, (iii) Present level of development and capacity to absorb credit, (iv) Concentration of SCs and STs population and other weaker sections living below the poverty line; and (v) Any other specific criteria which will facilitate optimum utilisation of available resources.

The cluster of villages selected are then allotted to the nearest Commercial and Co-operative Banks. The cluster of villages allotted could be adopted by the concerned bank branches not only under IRDP but also under other schemes.

Selection of Schemes

Depending on the local resource profile, schemes broadly falling in the area of agriculture and allied activities, village and cottage industries and service sector are identified for each block/village. The main schemes are divided into seven groups, agriculture, animal husbandry, minor irrigation, fisheries, social forestry and industries, services and business. They are further divided into several sub-groups.

It is essential that specific income generating scheme is entrusted to each identified beneficiary family. The identification of a scheme is done in full consultation of the beneficiary household concerned so that the scheme is appropriate to its inclination and management capability. If the scheme is to generate adequate net income to enable the household to cross the poverty line, it must be location specific with forward and backward linkages.

District and Block Level Planning

Identification of income generating schemes require intensive exercise of local resource analysis and planning. Two types of plans—one for the District and the other for Blocks—are required to be formulated for a meaningful implementation of the programme. The first is *'the perspective or indicative plans'* and the second *'The Annual Action Plans'*. The role of the perspective plan is to give indications about the local resource profile for preparation of annual action plans.

The perspective plans are required to be prepared at the block level which should be aggregated at the district level. These plans should ordinarily contain the following information:

(i) An inventory of local resources which may include the following information: *(a)* demographic trends and human resources, *(b)* areas and location-specific resources data, *(c)* economic activities with details of institutions engaged in these activities and *(d)* social and institutional infrastructure including the status of voluntary action groups;

(ii) Information regarding the ongoing programmes, both under plan and non-plan schemes. It should contain an analysis of the potential of these programmes in terms of offering opportunities for economically viable activities either through generation of direct employment opportunities or through provision of backward and forward linkages and infrastructural support;

(iii) Assessment of the likely activities under the programmes of the development departments in the next five years;

(iv) Impact of the IRDP activities so far undertaken on the economic environment.

The information is sought to be analysed to give broad indications regarding sector(s) of the economy which are capable of throwing up further employment opportunities. It may also be used to identify gaps in infrastructure and the developments and the programmes to fill up these gaps.

Annual Action Plan is an exercise which should succeed the perspective plan and the identification of beneficiaries. This plan has to match with the resource profile and the needs of the beneficiaries to provide them, income generating activities. The Annual Action Plan has to contain the following details:

(i) economic profile of the block/district spelling out the sectors proposed to be adopted giving reasons for the same;

(ii) the beneficiary family profile, broadly categorising them according to their aptitudes and choices for the income generating schemes and the scheme actually prepared for them. It should also give reasons if schemes different from their preferences, if any, are assigned;

(iii) the areas of coordination with the other departments and the extent of the involvement of other agencies and departments;

(iv) sources and mechanism for procurement of raw materials and disposal of finished goods;

(v) linkages with the DPAP, DDP, RLEGP, NREP, Land Reforms, MNP and SC Component and Tribal Development Plans and the infrastructural support drawn from these programmes;

(vi) an overall assessment of the impact of the proposed activities on the incomes of the assisted families and the economy of the area.

Implementation Machinery

The administration set up of IRDP at different levels is stated briefly hereunder. At the Central level, the Department of Rural Development in the Ministry of Agriculture, Government of India has overall responsibility for policy formulation, monitoring and evaluation of the programme.

At the State level, the Department of Rural Development (or any other department which looks after the Rural Development) is responsible for planning, implementation, monitoring and evaluation of the programme. A State level Co-ordination Committee with 12 members has been provided to assist this Department.

At the district level, the programme is implemented by the District Rural Development Agency (DRDA) with District Collector as Chairman and a full time project officer who is responsible for planning, project formulation and implementation of the programme. This agency is provided with a team of administrative monitoring and accounting staff besides Assistant Project Officers related to relevant fields in the area.

The main functions of DRDA includes, inter alia:

(i) To keep the district and block level agencies informed of basic parameters, requirements of the programme and the tasks to be performed by all these agencies;

(ii) To co-ordinate and oversee the surveys, preparation of perspective plans and Annual Action Plans of the blocks and finally prepare a district plan;

(iii) To evaluate and monitor the programme to ensure its effectiveness;

(iv) To secure inter-sectoral and inter-departmental co-ordination and co-operation;

(v) To give publicity to the achievements made under the programme and disseminate knowledge and build up awareness about the programme;

(vi) To send periodical returns to the State Government in the prescribed formats.

In the Sixth Plan the DRDAs were required to submit the annual plans to the State Level Co-ordination Committee for approval, these powers have now been delegated in the Seventh Plan to the governing body of the DRDA. The DRDAs are required to approve their annual plans by February and to start implementation from 1st April each year. This delegation has enabled the DRDAs to more effectively plan and implement the programme.

At the Block level, BDO (Now in Mandals, Mandal Development Officer—MDO) is responsible for the implementation of the programme. He is assisted by a number of Extension Officers and Village Development Officers (VDOs) in the block. At the grass root level, the VDO/VLW is responsible for proper implementation of the programme.

Provision of Subsidies and Credit

The beneficiary households are assisted, as has already been stated, through economically viable and technically feasible schemes which are financed partly by subsidies and partly by institutional credit. The amount of subsidy depends on two factors: the nature of the scheme and the category of the beneficiary household. Subsidies for individual families vary from 25 per cent to 50 per cent of the capital cost of the project. Small farmers are eligible for subsidy of 25 per cent of the total cost of the scheme. All other categories of beneficiaries, i.e., marginal farmers agricultural labourers are eligible for subsidy of 33 1/3 per cent. A family could be provided a maximum of Rs. 3,000 by way of subsidy, but the beneficiaries selected in drought prone area will get a maximum subsidy of Rs. 4,000. Scheduled Caste beneficiaries are now eligible to receive 50 per cent (30 per cent in Seventh Plan) subsidy under IRDP as in the case of ST beneficiaries subject to a maximum of Rs. 5,000. There is no monetary ceiling on subsidy (though percentage ceilings apply) for minor irrigation projects under the programme for old as well as new families.

The balance of the project cost has to be provided by the financial institutions—Commercial Banks, Regional Rural Banks and Cooperatives—as term loans. The effective implementation of IRDP depends largely on the smooth flow of credit from financial institutions, since credit is a key input in creation of productive assets, for promotion of self-employment and in achieving rapid diffusion of benefits of new technology. Subsidy granted by the Government is released to the financing institution which provides the balance of the project cost. The disbursement of subsidy and loan to the beneficiaries is made in kind. However, a pilot scheme of disbursement in cash is introduced in April 1987 in 22 blocks. Subsequently, the scheme is extended to 50 blocks from January 1990. With the launching of direct poverty alleviation programme for the rural poor, the banking policy is reoriented to make it supportive of the IRDP and other allied poverty eradication programmes. The credit needs of rural development programmes are of such a magnitude that multi-agency approach is adopted. There are two components of this approach: *(a)* commercial banks and the Regional Rural Banks, and *(b)* cooperatives. Their operations are guided and coordinated and supported by the recently established National Bank for Agriculture and Rural Development (NABARD). This new institution has taken over the role which earlier Reserve Bank of India used to play in regard to direction of provision of credit.

For better co-ordination with the banks, there is a four-tier mechanism. At the national level, there is a High Level Committee on Credit Support for IRDP under the Chairmanship of Secretary, Department of Rural Development. The committee includes representatives of Reserve Bank of India (RBI), NABARD, Commercial Banks, State Governments, Planning Commission, Banking and Insurance Divisions of Ministry of Finance and Ministry of Industry. This committee provides a forum to consider various problems and to review the credit arrangements and recommend changes and improvements.

Similarly, State level and District level committees have been constituted to monitor the flow of credit and to resolve bottlenecks in implementation at the grassroot level. At the cutting-edge level of the block also, consultative committees have been set up for bringing about coordination between the banks and officials working at that level.

Simultaneous with the efforts made at the administrative level to ensure coordination with the banking sector it is necessary for the Department of Rural Development to have a say in various banking forums. Accordingly, the Secretary, Department of Rural Development is a member of the High Level Standing Committee constituted by the RBI to review the flow of credit for IRDP. He is also a member of the Board of Directors of NABARD. Representatives of the Department of Rural Development are also associated with various working groups set up by the RBI, NABARD and Ministry of Finance on subjects concerning bank credit.

Any activity taken up under the IRDP really constitutes an economic project for the family. For the bank, its economic viability is crucial. To enable the poor family a fair opportunity of getting quality asset, the cost of the project given to him is crucial. NABARD has set up Regional Unit Cost Committees which are to meet twice in a year, review existing unit costs and to revise them, based upon the local situation.

Documentation is an important ingredient of the process of providing credit under IRDP. To facilitate this process the organisation of credit camps and credit-cum-recovery camps have been organised by the State Governments. The main aim of credit camps is to facilitate early completion of formalities required for sanction of loans and to avoid hardship to the beneficiaries. Camps are also used for contacting the IRDP beneficiaries for recovery of loans and to check whether the assets acquired have been put to proper use.

A major criticism of the programme was release of funds towards the end of the financial year and the bunching of application in the last quarter. Timely release of funds is a Sine quo non to good implementation. Since 1987-88, it has been ensured that the first of two instalments under IRDP are released to the DRDAs on the very first working day of the financial year.

Some important changes have been introduced in the procedure of financing by banks in 1987. Earlier, various banks used to have different application forms for IRDP loans. Some times, the same bank had different forms for activities. This created a lot of confusion and difficulty. To overcome this, with effect from 1st April 1987 a simplified application-cum-appraisal form for all banks and all activities under IRDP has been introduced. The limit for security-free loans under IRDP for activities under agriculture and allied sectors has been raised from Rs. 5,000 to Rs. 10,000.

As a special case it has been decided that monetary ceilings for subsidy under IRDP in the pilot districts would be relaxed as follows: *(a)* The ceiling of subsidy limit is Rs. 4,000 in non-DPAP areas, Rs. 5,000 in DPAP areas and Rs. 6,000 in case of SC and ST families *(b)* the Reserve Bank of India (RBI) has been requested to waive security requirements for loans over Rs. 10,000 and to allow banks to charge 10 per cent interest on par with IRDP even for loans over Rs. 7,500. These concessions will only be applicable to 200 families selected for the pilot project in the designated districts in the year 1991-92.

In order to provide social security to the IRDP families, a Group Life Insurance Scheme has been started from 1st April 1988 through Life Insurance Corporation (LIC) of India. Under this scheme, every IRDP beneficiary assisted after 1st April 1988 will be insured for a period of three years. As per the revised rules all IRDP beneficiaries of not less than 18 years and not more than 60 years will be covered. The age of beneficiaries as registered in records of the DRDA shall be admitted by LIC for this purpose. In case of death, the family would receive a sum of Rs. 3,000 with double benefit in the case of accidental death. The entire premium for this scheme is being shared equally by the Central and State Government and the beneficiaries need not have to pay towards premium cost.[6]

Follow-up and Monitoring

The Ministry of Rural Development has rightly laid great stress on adequate follow-up action and monitoring of the programme for its effective implementation. Monitoring provides the necessary information through an effective feedback process to enable the management of the project to know how the programme is running and to take corrective measures for effective programme implementation. It helps to know whether (i) the inputs of the programme are properly delivered (ii) the use of inputs are according to programme intentions and (iii) the inputs are able to produce initial impacts as desired. Monitoring, therefore, is exclusively an internal tool for controlling and supervising programme implementation. For this purpose, an identify-cum-monitoring card called *'Vikas Patrika'*, is given to each beneficiary. Copies of this document are to be supplied to the banks and also maintained at the block and DRDA levels. The project officers of DRDA and BDOs/MDOs assign the responsibility for filling up the monitoring card, along with its updating and inspection. A monitoring schedule is to be drawn up indicating the names of the functionaries responsible for monitoring and particular days are fixed for their visits. This is done to ensure that the beneficiaries have maintained the assets properly and have derived benefits therefrom. It will also to act as a check that the assets have not been disposed of fraudulently. The follow-up has to be done for a minimum period of 2 to 3 years after the assets are acquired by the beneficiaries. In this way, the State Government will be able to find out the exact number of families assisted and those who have crossed the poverty line. For proper follow-up and post-credit supervision, the village functionaries are asked to adopt one village. They are expected to call on the beneficiaries every fortnight and depending upon the fact whether assets are with the beneficiaries or not, they were required to send a green card as the case may be, to the BDO/MDO and Project Officer, DRDA. Accordingly, the BDO/MDO or the Project Officer are required to take corrective action immediately. The Project Officers are also required to report by the tenth of every month about the compliance of action calender to the Secretary, Special Schemes Organisation (SSO). The progress is also being reviewed at the levels of Ministers and the Chief Minister periodically.

There is a Monitoring Cell in each DRDA under the charge of an Assistant Project Officer (APO, Monitoring) who is normally assisted by two economic/statistical assistants in the preparation of periodic progress reports.

At the State level, there is a coordination committee to provide guidance to DRDAs in monitoring of the IRDP and to secure inter-departmental coordination and linkages for the programme. The Department of Rural Development at the State level provides the requisite administrative support. A full-fledged Monitoring Cell under the charge of an officer of the rank of Joint Director is provided at the State level. The management control at the State level is also mainly through progress reports, periodic review meetings and field visits.

At the Central level, the Department of Rural Development in the Ministry of Agriculture is responsible for policy planning, framing and periodic revision of guidelines and for ensuring the effective implementation of the programme throughout the country. A Central Committee on IRDP with Union Secretary as Chairman oversees the major policy matters. Again, the management control of the Centre is through progress reports, review meetings and field visits. Another effective tool of management control by the Centre is, of course, the control on release of funds.

From the foregoing paragraphs, it is evident that there are four levels of management in the planning and implementation of IRDP, viz., Centre, State, DRDA and Block Office. Except for Block Office, the other management levels have only remote control over the implementation of the programme. The major instrument of this remote control is periodic progress reports. Over the years, fairly efficient Management Information System (MIS) has been developed for this purpose.

A general principle of MIS for monitoring is that it has to be pyramidical in shape. As the information moves upwards towards higher levels of management it becomes thinner. There is hardly any evidence of detailed analysis of periodic progress reports at the DRDA and State levels with a view to taking corrective/supportive actions for improving the implementation of the programme. But, then exceptions are always there; some of the DRDA project directors have been very effectively using the MIS for closely monitoring the implementation of the programme with much beneficial results. Some had even taken initiative on their own in computerised MIS. Indeed, the impetus for introducing computerised Rural Information Systems Project (CRISP) came from the personal initiatives of a few such officers. This project now covers the entire country.

A major limitation of the monitoring arrangement at the lower and middle management in the case of IRDP is that the data collection and information generation are conditioned by the requirements for progress reports to higher authorities rather than for using as a management tool at the appropriate level. And often the data/information are not available to the functional managers at various levels. For example, the progress reports prepared in the Monitoring Cell by APO, Monitoring, are often not available to the other APOs of the DRDA who are in charge of various sectoral activities. Indeed, almost invariably the information relating to progress or problems relating to implementation move vertically upwards only; very rarely they flow horizontally or vertically downwards. Because of such information gaps, quite often inter-departmental and even intra-departmental coordination in planning and execution of the projects has been lacking. Another serious limitation of the existing monitoring arrangements is that it is essentially an input-oriented rather than output-oriented monitoring system. Most of the key performance indicators used for monitoring of IRDP and input indicators. They essentially deal with financial utilisation and physical achievements in numbers. Since the targets are expressed in terms of these indicators, achievements are measured in terms of the same indicators. Higher the amount spent, the better and higher the number of families assisted. There is hardly any indicator to assess the quality of assistance or the outcome of the project. Even when qualitative information are required, they are often presented in quantitative terms. In fact, this infatuation with numbers in progress reporting, at times, reaches comical proportions. Often by thinly spreading assistance over large number of beneficiaries, the progress achieved overshoots the target, but only at great cost in terms of quality of assistance.[7]

Review of Progress of IRDP

The quantitative spread of the programme has been significant. The performance of IRDP during the Sixth and Seventh Plan periods is shown in Tables—2.1 and 2.2. *(See page 43 and 45).*

The performance of IRDP during the Sixth Plan (Table—2.1) shows that at the national level the targets have been achieved in respect of all the quantitative parameters set out in the programme guidelines. The total allocation of funds for the programme during the period was Rs. 1,766.81 crores as against the target of Rs. 1,500 crores of which the allocation of the Centre was Rs. 901.08 crores. The total expenditure incurred was Rs. 1,661.17 crores as against the target of Rs. 1,500 crores. The total credit provided by financial institutions amounted to Rs. 3,101.61 crores. The Sixth Plan target was to assist 150 lakh beneficiaries over the period. The actual number of families assisted was 165.82 lakhs which surpassed the target. The SC/ST beneficiaries covered was 64.63 lakhs as against the target of 50 lakhs, i.e. 39.02 per cent. It thus exceeded the stipulated percentage of 30 per cent. The per capita subsidy provided was Rs. 1,103 while the per capita credit given was Rs. 1,873. It was complained that the financial assistance provided per scheme had fallen short of the scheme cost. As can be seen from 2.1 the performance of the programme was satisfactory during the Sixth Plan period. Evaluation studies made by some well-known organisations as sponsored by the Planning Commission in 1982-84 indicated that additional income had accrued in the case of majority of the assisted families. However, the percentage of those rising above the prescribed poverty threshold of Rs. 3,500 per annum did not exceed 40.[8]

Table—2.1

Performance of IRDP in the Sixth Plan (1980-85)

Sl. No.	*Item*	*Unit*	*Target*	*Achievement*
1.	Total allocation	Rs. Crores	1500.00	1766.81
2.	Central allocation	Rs. Crores	750.00	901.08
3.	Central releases	Rs. Crores	750.00	788.39
4.	Total expenditure	Rs. Crores	1500.00	1661.17
5.	Total term credit mobilised	Rs. Crores	3000.00	3101.61
6.	Total investment	Rs. Crores	4500.00	4762.78
7.	Total number of beneficiaries covered	Lakh Nos.	150.00	165.82
8.	Number of SC/ST beneficiaries covered	Lakh Nos.	50.00	64.63
9.	Per capita subsidy	Rs.	1000.00	1103.00
10.	Per capita credit	Rs.	2000.00	1873.00
11.	Per capita investment	Rs.	3000.00	2876.00
12.	Subsidy-credit ratio		1:2	1:1.87

Source : RBI: A Review of the Agricultural Credit System in India, Report of the Agricultural Credit Review Committee, Reserve Bank of India, Bombay, 1989, p. 746.

In the Seventh Five Year Plan the poverty line for the rural areas was enhanced to Rs. 6,400 from Rs. 3,500. By keeping the cut off point for identification at Rs. 4,800, the plan emphasized giving priority to those families with an annual income of Rs. 3,500. The programme guidelines for the Seventh Plan emphasized a higher investment by each family than that of Rs. 3,339 in 1984-85, the last year of the Sixth Plan. Unless the average level of investment is more than Rs. 5,000, the families cannot cross the poverty level. But this level was not attained in the Seventh Plan period. Although some beneficiaries assisted during the Sixth Plan period derived incremental income from the asset, that income was not sufficient to enable them to cross the poverty line. Hence a supplementary dose of assistance was provided to such families during the Seventh Plan, provided they are not wilful defaulters. Even the assistance so provided proved to be insufficient to enable the families to cross the poverty line. Another defect of the Sixth Plan approach was a uniform target of 600 families to be assisted each year in each block and uniform outlay of Rs. 35 lakhs per block which was changed in the Seventh Plan. The incidence of poverty was taken into account when allocating financial resources for each State. For the first time in June 1985, a separate target of 20 per cent women was fixed which was raised to 30 per cent in August, 1985.

The data given in Table—2.2 enables one to understand the progress achieved during the Seventh Plan period. The Seventh Plan has provided a larger public sector allocation for this programme as the planners seem to feel that a revamped programme would be a very significant device for poverty alleviation in rural areas. The achievements in respect of total allocations and central release of funds have exceeded the target. The total allocation of funds for the programme was Rs. 3,000.27 crores as against the target of Rs. 2,358.81 crores. The total expenditure incurred was Rs. 3,315.18 crores and the term credit mobilised was Rs. 5,372.53 crores. The number of families covered slightly fell short of the target. The SC/ST families assisted during the plan period had exceeded the stipulated percentage of 40. The percentage of women beneficiaries assisted (18.89) fallen short of the stipulated percentage of 30.

The per capita investment was Rs. 4,780. The per capita subsidy provided was Rs. 1,824 while the per capita credit given was Rs. 2,956. This level of investment also proved to be insufficient to enable the poorest of the poor to cross the poverty line. The Public Accounts Committee, therefore, suggested in April, 1987 an average assistance of Rs. 7,000 to Rs. 9,000 per family.

Table—2.2
Performance of IRDP in the Seventh Plan (1985–90)

Sl. No.	*Items*	*Unit*	*Target*	*Achievement*
1.	Total allocation	Rs. Crores	2358.81	3000.27
2.	Central allocation	Rs. Crores	1186.79	1513.84
3.	Central releases	Rs. Crores	—	1465.26
4.	Total expenditure	Rs. Crores	—	3315.81
5.	Total term-credit mobilised	Rs. Crores	—	5372.53
6.	Total investment	Rs. Crores	4000.00	8688.34
7.	Total number of families covered			
	Old	Lakh Nos.	100.00	51.80
	New	Lakh Nos.	100.00	129.97
	Total	Lakh Nos.	200.00	
8.	Number of SC/ST beneficiaries covered	Lakh Nos.	—	81.87
9.	Number of women beneficiaries covered	Lakh Nos.	—	34.33
10.	Per capita subsidy (Gross)	Rs.	—	1824.00
11.	Per capita credit (Gross)	Rs.	—	2956.00
12.	Per capita investment (Gross)	Rs.	—	4780.00
13.	Subsidy-credit Ratio		1:2	1:1.98*

Note* : Net subsidy-credit ratio.

Source : Planning Commission, Eighth Five Year Plan (1992-97), Vol. II, Government of India, New Delhi, p. 48.

Table—2.2 also shows that along with the steady increase in the number of beneficiaries covered and quantum of bank credit disbursed has also increased. The data show that the performance of banks in providing IRDP loans is quite satisfactory. Considering the importance of this programme and the refinance facility available from the NABARD, they are expected to participate effectively particularly when the Government of India has also increased the risk fund contribution to 6 per cent for all loans given to IRDP beneficiaries.

The extent of coverage of SC/STs (1980-81 to 1989-90) and women (1985-86 to 1989-90) beneficiaries under IRDP are given in Table—2.3.

Table—2.3
Coverage of SCs and STs and Women Beneficiaries Under IRDP

(in Lakh)

Sl. No.	*Year*	*Total beneficiaries*	*SC and ST beneficiaries*	*% of SC & ST in the Total*	*Women beneficiaries*	*% of Women in the Total*
1.	1980-81	27.27	7.81	28.64	–	–
2.	1981-82	27.13	10.01	36.90	–	–
3.	1982-83	34.55	14.06	40.69	–	–
4.	1983-84	36.85	15.37	41.71	–	–
5.	1984-85	39.82	17.38	43.65	–	–
6.	1985-86	30.60	13.23	43.23	3.03	9.90
7.	1986-87	37.47	16.80	44.84	5.67	15.13
8.	1987-88	42.47	18.99	47.71	8.30	19.54
9.	1988-89	37.72	17.50	46.39	8.74	23.17
10.	1989-90	33.51	15.45	46.11	8.59	25.63

Source : 1. Government of India, The Seventh Five Year Plan, 1985-90, Vol. II, Planning Commission, New Delhi, October, 1985, pp. 52-53.

2. Government of India, Annual Report, 1989-90, Department of Rural Development, Ministry of Agriculture, New Delhi, p. 23.

It is observed from Table—2.3 that the coverage of SC and ST beneficiaries under IRDP has continuously increased from 28.64 per cent in the year 1980-81 to 47.71 per cent in the year 1987-88. There was a small decline in the last two years (1987-88 and 1989-90). However, the achievement is higher than the target fixed for them. The coverage of women beneficiaries gradually increased from 9.89 per cent in the year 1985-86 to 25.63 per cent in the year 1989-90. These achievements indicate the importance given to SC/ST and also women to improve their levels of living.

Sector-wise coverage of schemes under IRDP during 1980-81 to 1989-90 are given in Table—2.4.

Table—2.4
Sector-wise Coverage of Beneficiaries under IRDP
(Percentage)

Sl. No.	*Year*	*Primary Sector*	*Secondary Sector*	*Tertiary Sector*	*Total*
1.	1980-81	93.56	2.32	4.12	100.00
2.	1981-82	83.02	4.92	12.06	100.00
3.	1982-83	68.70	15.70	15.60	100.00
4.	1983-84	58.90	13.20	27.90	100.00
5.	1984-85	54.50	15.70	29.80	100.00
6.	1985-86	48.62	17.18	34.20	100.00
7.	1986-87	45.30	18.55	36.15	100.00
8.	1987-88	41.16	18.54	40.30	100.00
9.	1988-89	41.81	19.32	38.87	100.00
10.	1989-90	43.05	19.39	37.56	100.00

Source : 1. Government of India, The Seventh Five Year Plan, 1985-90, Vol. II, Planning Commission, New Delhi, October, 1985, pp. 52-53.

2. Government of India, Annual Report, 1989-90, Department of Rural Development, Ministry of Agriculture, New Delhi, p. 23.

Table—2.4 shows that there has been some shift in the nature of productive activities/schemes being undertaken by the beneficiaries. The percentage of beneficiaries assisted in the primary sector decreased from 93.56 per cent in 1980-81 to 41.61 per cent in the year 1987-88. But in the last two years (1988-89 and 1989-90) it showed an increase. In the secondary sector the percentage of beneficiaries increased from 2.32 per cent in the year 1980-81 to 15.7 per cent in the year 1982-83. In the year 1983-84 it decreased to 13.2 per cent. After that it gradually increased from 15.7 per cent in 1984-85 to 19.39 per cent by 1989-90. In the tertiary sector it increased from 4.12 per cent in the year 1980-81 to 40.30 per cent in the year 1987-88.

There was a slight reduction in the last two years of the period. All the data provided above will clearly indicate that there has been diversification of schemes from the primary to secondary and service sectors. As a matter of fact, the programme seeks to promote a greater coverage of families under secondary and tertiary sectors. This constitutes an encouraging trend in the rural economy.

Before we leave this chapter, we describe the two supportive programmes of IRDP and the Wage Employment Programmes which are intended to benefit the rural poor.

SUPPORTIVE PROGRAMMES TO IRDP

National Rural Employment Programme (NREP)

During the Sixth Five Year Plan, the National Rural Employment Programme was initiated to create additional employment opportunities to the rural poor for gainful employment during the lean agricultural season with an outlay of Rs. 980 crores for the Plan period. There was a provision in the State plans for this programme from 1981-82 onwards as it is being operated on 50:50 sharing basis. This included the provision of Rs. 1,509.22 crores for rural development programme in State Plans. In order to ensure that benefits of this programme reach the weaker sections of the society, at least 10 per cent of the allocation under the programme was earmarked for utilisation exclusively on programme of direct benefit to Scheduled Castes viz., drinking water wells, community irrigation schemes in which the majority of the beneficiaries are harijans, environmental improvement works in Harijan localities and house sites/group housing for the Harijans. The programme gained momentum in 1978-79 when over 12 lakh tonnes of food grains were utilised for creating 372.8 million mandays of employment. The programme besides creating substantial additional employment in the rural areas during the lean employment periods, more particularly in areas affected by the widespread drought of 1979 has made a favourable impact on stabilisation of wages in the rural areas and also helped to check the rise in prices of food grains. The operation of this programme on a year-to-year basis resulted in uncertainty about its continuance for the full plan period. During the Seventh Plan period Rs. 901.84 crores was spent under NREP upto the end of 1988-89 and against the target of 3,427 lakhs mandays 3,796 mandays of employment was generated.

Training of Rural Youth for Self Employment (TRYSEM)

A new programme to train rural youth for self employment (TRYSEM) was also initiated with the objective of providing technical skills to rural youth to enable them to take up self employment in the rural areas in the fields of agriculture and allied activities, industries, services and business activities. The Sixth Plan aimed to train 2 lakh rural youths every year at the rate of 40 youths drawn from each block. It was also indicated that a minimum of 30 per cent of the trained youth should belong to Scheduled Castes and Scheduled Tribes communities and a minimum 1/3rd of the total rural youth trained should be women. During the Seventh Plan period Rs. 152.41 crores was spent to train the youth.

Rural Landless Employment Guarantee Programme (RLEGP)

The Rural Landless Employment Guarantee Programme was introduced in 1983 with the objectives of improving and expanding employment opportunities for the rural landless with a view to provide employment to at least one member of every landless household upto 100 days in a year and creating durable assets for strengthening the infrastructure so as to meet the growing requirements of the rural economy.

However, during the Seventh Plan, amount of Rs. 2,411.98 crores was spent in the Central Sector and generated 2,794 million mandays of employment upto the end of 1989.

Development of Women and Children in Rural Areas (DWCRA)

A separate programme for rural women was considered necessary as it was noticed that they were not availing of the benefits of IRDP due to various social constraints. The programme of DWCRA was therefore started in September 1982 as a sub-scheme of IRDP. The programme has its focus on rural households with women as head of the family and women members of rural families below the poverty line. To motivate women to come forward to take up income generating activities for supplementing their family income, the strategy of group formation was adopted for DWCRA. Women belonging to target families can avail of loan and subsidy under IRDP and also become members of DWCRA groups.[9]

DWCRA was initially launched as a pilot measure in 50 selected districts. In selecting the districts, priority is given to those rate so with low female literacy and high infant mortality that the most backward sections of rural population can derive the benefits.[10] As on 31st March 1991 it was being implemented in 187 districts all over the country. It is proposed to cover the remaining districts during the Eighth Plan. The salient features of the programme are: *(a)* Identified women are organised into groups, each consisting of about 10-15 women, *(b)* Skill training is imparted to the members before they take up an economic activity, *(c)* Any viable activity can be taken up under DECRA, *(d)* Each DWCRA group is given a one time grant of Rs. 15,000 as revolving fund for infrastructure, purchase of raw materials, marketing, child care, etc., *(e)* The amount of revolving fund is contributed in equal shares by Government of India, the State

Government and United Nations International Children's Emergency Fund (UNICEF).

The Sixth Plan outlay for the scheme was Rs. 15.60 crores in addition to UNICEF assistance of Rs. 5.40 crores. During the Sixth Plan (1980-85), in all 3,308 groups covering 52,170 women beneficiaries were organised and the total expenditure was Rs. 162.15 lakhs. Over 28,000 groups were formed during the Seventh Plan, against the target of 30,000 groups. In the same plan period an amount of Rs. 36.63 crores was utilised as against the outlay of Rs. 48.05 crores, out of which Rs. 20.30 crores is Central Share.

To sustain the interest of women in the programme, their activities are to be economically viable. Marketing of products made by women's groups, therefore, assumes importance. Several steps have been taken in this direction. Some State Governments have issued orders declaring DWCRA group as approved source for supply of bulk articles required by Government departments. Household items are being marketed under brand names. Facilities offered by State Government emporia, public sector corporations and women's development corporations are utilised for display and sale of DWCRA products. A comprehensive evaluation of DWCRA was done through a reputed research agency. The report has thrown light on the positive impact of the programme on the target population. At the same time, it has also drawn attention to various weaknesses and constraints. Necessary corrective steps are being taken to make the programme more meaningful.

Wage Employment Programmes

The Wage Employment Schemes are (National Rural Employment Programme, Rural Landless Employment Guarantee Programme, Indira Awaas Yojana, Million Wells Scheme and Jawahar Rozgar Yojana) described hereunder.

Indira Awaas Yojana (IAY)

Indira Awaas Yojana which was an important component of RLEGP with effect from 1985-86, under which construction of dwelling units free of cost, for the poorest of the poor belonging to SCs and STs and freed bonded labourers. Houses under IAY, as far as possible, are to be built in clusters as per micro-habitat approach so that common facilities can be provided by the clusters. During the period 1985-86 to 1989-90, Rs. 759.89 crores were allocated for IAY. Against the target of constructing 7,47,257 houses, 6,87,839 houses were actually constructed involving an expenditure of Rs. 677.43 crores. During 1990-91 also, an allocation of Rs. 157.38 crores has been made for IAY with a target of 1,22,100 houses. As per reports received so far, 90,663 houses have been constructed at a cost of Rs. 97.28 crores.[11] From 1989-90 it was implemented under Jawahar Rozgar Yojana.

Million Wells Scheme (MWS)

The Million Wells Scheme launched during 1988-89 with the objective of providing open irrigation wells free of cost to poor small and marginal farmers belonging to SCs/STs and freed bonded labourers, as a sub scheme of NREP/RLEGP, is continued under JRY. In the year 1990-91, 20 per cent of the resources was earmarked for MWS. The State Governments are required to allocate MWS resources to the districts. The allocation is intended only for open wells. Where wells are not feasible due to geological factors, the funds allotted under MWS can be utilised for other schemes of minor irrigation like irrigation tanks are also for the development of land belonging to SCs/STs and freed bonded labourers including the ceiling surplus lands, Bhoodan land etc., allotted to them.

During 1989-90, no separate earmarking for MWS was made. However, construction of open wells was permitted against 15 per cent earmarked allocation for SCs/STs of the district level funds. During 1990-91, 20 per cent of the total allocation has been earmarked for MWS.[12] During the period 1988-89 and 1990-91, 1,48,986 wells were completed involving an expenditure of Rs. 207.63 crores.

Jawahar Rozgar Yojana (JRY)

In 1989, NREP and RLEGP were merged into a single and expanded new programme called the Jawahar Rozgar Yojana

(Jawahar employment programme, thus named after India's first Prime Minister Jawaharlal Nehru whose birth centenary was celebrated during 1988-89).[13] The primary objective of the programme is generation of additional gainful employment for the unemployed and under-employed in the rural areas, the secondary objective is creation of sustained employment by strengthening the rural economic infrastructure and assets and improvement in the overall quality of life in rural areas. The salient features of the programme are *(a)* expenditure under the programme shared between the Centre and States in the ratio of 80:20, *(b)* Central assistance released to the States. State Governments are required to release the grants to DRDAs/Zilla Parishads within a week after the release of Central assistance along with their own matching share, *(c)* preference to SCs/STs and freed bonded labour for employment, *(d)* 30 per cent of employment opportunities reserved for women, *(e)* resources of two or more districts/village panchayats can be pooled to take up works for common benefit of the concern districts/village panchayats, *(f)* works can be taken up for execution during any part of the year whenever the need for generating employment is felt, preferably during the lean agricultural season, *(g)* in those States which give foodgrains as part of wages, 1.5 kg., of foodgrains is given to the workers at subsidised rates, *(h)* contractors or middlemen are not permitted to be engaged for executing any of the works, *(i)* at least 60 per cent of the resources have to be spent as wage component, *(j)* amount upto a maximum of 2 per cent of annual allocation is allowed to be spent on administrative/contingent expenditure at State/ District/Block/Village Panchayat level. DRDAs/ZPs can spend upto a maximum of Rs. 50,000 on training of officials/non-officials involved in the implementation of JRY at the District/ Block/Village Panchayat level.[14]

During the period 1989-90 and 1990-91, a target of 18,048.29 lakh mandays has been fixed against which the achievement was 17,321.38 lakh mandays.[15] In the same period, an amount of Rs. 5,013.32 crores was utilised as against the outlay of Rs. 4,200 crores.[16]

CONCLUSIONS

The first two decades of planning revealed that the impact of a growth-oriented development strategy did not *'trickle down'* to the poorest of the poor. A strategy of direct attack on the incidence of poverty was first articulated in India towards the mid 1970s at the time of the formulation of the Fifth Five Year Plan. This strategy envisaged a quantitative target for the reduction in the incidence of poverty through improvement in the level of consumption of the poor. This plan postulated a specific type of production structure in order to achieve the desired pattern of household consumption of commodities and services among the different strata of the population. Unfortunately, however, this strategy could not be fully implemented due to the shock exerted by the steep rise in oil prices in 1973 and the consequent problems of structural adjustment which emerged in the economy. From the late 1970s onwards, especially during the 1980s, various types of policies have been implemented for reducing the incidence of poverty. It was in this context that the IRDP was born.

The Integrated Rural Development Programme has been the centre place of the poverty alleviation measures implemented from Sixth Five Year Plan. The implementation of IRDP, TRYSEM, DWCRA, NREP and RLEGP during the last seven to ten years and the large number of studies to evaluate these programmes in different parts of the country have enabled a national consensus to emerge in favour of continuing a package consisting of self-employment and wage-employment programmes.

IRDP has been evaluated by a number of organisations, research institutions and individual scholars in recent years. The studies on the working of IRDP reveal that generally the number of assisted persons who would have crossed the poverty line *"would not exceed around 40 per cent"*. Our former Prime Minister, late Shri Rajiv Gandhi also had himself openly declared to the press that 80 per cent allotted money under IRDP went into wrong hands and only 20 per cent reached the beneficiaries. This aspect, apart from underlining the need to remedy the shortcomings of the programme, arouses interest on an understanding of the general impact of IRDP on beneficiaries. The present study is an attempt in this direction.

REFERENCES

1. The World Bank, *'Focus on Poverty'*, World Development Report, Oxford University Press, 1990, p. 29.

2. Planning Commission, *Draft Five Year Plan (1978-83)*, Government of India, p. 154.

3. J.C. Adyar and J.P. Lahoti, *'Ensuring Genuine Rural Development'*, Kurukshetra, Vol. XXVIII, No. 15, May, 1; 1980, p. 4.

4. Uma Lele, *'The Design of Rural Development Lessons from Africa'*, The Johns Hopkins University Press, London, 1975, p. 20.

5. Krishnaswami, O.R., *"Strategy of IRDP"*, Kurukshetra, Vol. XXXIII, No. 11, August, 1985, p. 5.

6. Inderjit Khanna, *"Integrated Rural Development Programme—Strategy for self-employment opportunities"*, Journal of Rural Development, Vol. 9, No. 1, 1990, pp. 41-42.

7. Kurien, N.J., *"Monitoring and Evaluation of Poverty Alleviation Programmes—Some conceptual and methodological issues"* Journal of Rural Development, Vol. 9, No. 1, 1990, pp. 197-208.

8. Planning Commission, *Seventh Five Year Plan, 1985-90*, Government of India, pp. 52-53.

9. Government of India, *Annual Report (1990-91)*, Department of Rural Development, Ministry of Agriculture, New Delhi, p. 51.

10. *Ibid.*, p. 32.

11. Government of India (10), *Op. cit.*, pp. 39-40.

12. *Ibid.*, p. 39.

13. Montek S. Ahluwalia, *"Policies for Poverty Alleviation"*, Asian Development Review, Vol. 8, No. 8, 1990, pp. 111-132.

14. Government of India (10), *Op. cit.*, p. 37.

15. Government of India (14), *Op. cit.*, p. 37.

16. Government of India (10), *Op. cit.*, pp. 63 & 66-69.

3

Review of Literature

The Integrated Rural Development Programme marked a distinct departure from the earlier plans in which poverty alleviation was counted largely on fruits of the overall economic growth. It is also concurrently evaluated by the Department of Rural Development. Evaluation is undertaken to know how the programme is being implemented and what can be done to remove the constraints, if any, encountered during the course of its implementation. Evaluation is thus a kind of achievement audit and mostly takes place after the programme ran for some specific period. In case of a long-term programme like IRDP, evaluation on continuous basis is restored to and such continuous evaluation at short intervals is known as concurrent evaluation.

It is desirable to review the relevant literature while handling a research problem. It shows what and how much work has already been done in the area under investigation. It also provides basis for identifying the research gaps and issues for further study. Many international and national economists have evaluated the Integrated Rural Development Programme. Paul Samuel,[1] in his international level study focussed on the objectives and the strategies of the IRDP and linked distributional impact, productivity of the investment and credit repayment to banking institutions as three critical components of success. D. Bandyopadhyay in his study[2] mainly focussed on income generation through asset endowment, and due to the death of the animal or owing to the lack of forward linkages and sheer pressure of poverty, the assisted beneficiary may again get deprived of the capital stock created for him. Unless a rehabilitation programme is built into the whole scheme, such nominal beneficiaries will be earmarked as defaulters in the banking system. Banking institutions have a crucial role to play as bankers are trained to handle a small number of large accounts and averse to dealing with a large number of small accounts. M.L. Dantwala in his study[3] on the Integrated Rural Development Programme, basically focussing on the philosophy of the policies and programme, stated that equity oriented policies and programmes pursued will not only be self defeating, but may prove counter-productive through a trickle up. More simply, a direct attack on poverty without an equal and direct attack on the structure has bred poverty. The IRDP has led to the total dependence of the poor on the employers. It has achieved very little and may have been misconceived, but this does not prove that the strategy of generating assets for the poor and upgrading their skills is wrong. Nilakantha Rath in his study[4] focussed on the main theme that the IRDP approach which is based on distribution of assets to the poor for creating self-employment is not going to deliver the goods. IRDP does not integrate resource-based or sectoral planning with household based planning and it is merely a household-based plan and this approach is not realistic. The subsidy element of IRDP had encouraged corruption in rural areas and has raised indebtedness of the poor in many cases. Hardly 18.70 per cent of the total beneficiaries have crossed the poverty line as IRDP strategy is largely misconceived.

The Institute of Financial Management and Research (IFMR)[5] has undertaken the study of IRDP, which is methodologically superior to the studies of NABARD and PEO, and collected data relating to 1,859 samples from 17 blocks in 3 district in Maharashtra and 2 districts in Tamil Nadu. Though this study restricted geographically, it was based on a much larger sampling fraction than NABARD and PEO studies. This study examines and economic position till February 1982, thus excluding the drought conditions of 1982-83. Like the two earlier studies, it also found that wrong identification, adoption of uniform strategy without considering the regional differences, disregarding the infrastructure availability, forward and backward linkages while selecting the activities, and unsound credit delivery system were the major defects in programme implementation. Though, by contrast, the IFMR study is methodologically superior, it allowed for only 15 months after the inception of the programme, and admittedly short period for the benefits to percolate. Robert V. Pulley in his study[6] at an all India level concluded that only 44 per cent of the disadvantaged beneficiaries have succeeded in maintaining the assets and repaying credit to banks. Poor households have faced difficulty in maintaining investment on assets. Investment must therefore, be tailored to the demands of the households, grounded in their own knowledge of the opportunity costs they face. The most important failure of the IRDP is its inability to ensure continued access to institutional credit for disadvantaged rural households.

An evaluation of IRDP in Southern States,[7] namely Andhra Pradesh, Tamil Nadu, Karnataka and Kerala was taken up by R.N. Tripathi and others at National Institute of Rural Development (NIRD). The survey was carried out in 1982 wherein beneficiaries of 1981-82 were covered. The objective of the comprehensive evaluation was to understand the pattern of income generation with respect to different schemes in different locations. A sample of 1,600 respondents were selected from all major schemes. In each state, four blocks were selected and in each block 100 beneficiaries were considered. The non-beneficiary respondents constituted 50 per cent of the sample and their distribution for the three levels of state, district and block followed the same principle as in the case of beneficiary respondents. The entire sample of beneficiary and non-beneficiary respondents taken together was 2,400.

B.C. Muthayya in his state level study[8] touched on the procedural aspects in the supply of loans to the beneficiaries under the IRDP and reported that there was an improvement in the per capita income subsequent to becoming the beneficiaries of the IRDP and also pointed out that the delay in getting loan and difficulty in providing the surety were the two main problems faced by a few beneficiaries.

The State Bank of India[9] has conducted two evaluation studies, the first in the latter half of 1984 covering 10 lead districts of the Bank in 9 States (a sample of 1,000 beneficiaries) and the second in 1985-86 covering 13 different districts in 12 States. Since the second study covered larger number of districts in more States with improved methodology, the findings of the second study are presented here. Out of the 13 districts selected, 9 are Bank's lead districts. The Study covered 1,295 beneficiaries assisted in the year 1982-83 and 1983-84.

N.J. Kurien in his study[10] while touching on the economic rationality and the viability of the IRDP and its effective execution has emphasised that nearly twenty per cent of the non-eligible beneficiaries who have an annual income of more than Rs. 3,500/- were identified and assisted under IRDP. Fifty five per cent of the beneficiaries had assets in the primary sector and 35 per cent in the tertiary sector. The government functionaries preferred to provide *"easily manageable"* assets to the beneficiaries irrespective of their income generating potential and in some cases even against the perference of the beneficiaries. Sixty eight per cent of the beneficiaries thought that the assets they got were not worth the cost.

The Concurrent Evaluation[11] Report for the period January-December 1987 shows that about 92 per cent of the assisted families indeed had pre-assistance income of less than Rs. 4,800. About 81 per cent of beneficiaries had found the assistance sufficient for acquiring assets. In 72 per cent cases, the assets were found intact. In the remaining cases some of the reasons for asset not being intact included unexpected events like death, illness (7 per cent), inadequate income generation (6 per cent), high maintenance cost (2 per cent), defective condition (4 per cent), compulsive household consumption requirements (1 per cent) and other reasons (6 per cent). As per this evaluation, about

60 per cent of old beneficiaries had crossed the poverty line of Rs. 3,500 and 13 per cent as per the revised poverty line of Rs. 6,400. This evaluation further supports the view that in about 77 per cent of cases the assets had generated incremental income.

Indira Hirway in her State level study[12] examined the adequacy of the target group approach in eradicating rural poverty and concluded that nearly 55 per cent to 75 per cent of the beneficiaries of IRDP are non-poor. The benefits received by the beneficiaries are not always substantial mainly due to a faulty design of the economics of the schemes. There is lack of understanding of the role which the highly stratified structure of the rural society plays in generating the forces.

Naidu and Rao's evaluation study[13] covered six blocks in Guntur District. The main aim of the study was evaluating the impact of IRDP schemes of generation of additional employment and income by different schemes is not identical. Of the five schemes studied, milch cattle, sheep rearing, minor irrigation, bullock and bullock carts and ISB schemes—the increase in number of additional mandays of employment is relatively higher in the case of ISB schemes compared to other schemes. With regard to the generation of additional income the minor irrigation scheme ranks high with an additional income of Rs. 359.60 followed by milch cattle scheme with 213.11 and ISB with Rs. 108.12 per family. The study concluded that revitalisation of the entire implementation process towards identifying and assisting those schemes which can shift the population from traditional sectors to employment oriented sectors is necessary and a careful analysis of local requirements and potentialities and preparation of plans on need based criterion would result in better implementation of IRDP.

Kutty Krishnan[14] conducted a case study on IRDP in Edakkad village of Cannanore district of Kerala during March and April 1984. The study covered 80 households who were assisted in the year 1982. The observations of the study was 20 per cent of the beneficiaries were eligible for the benefits under the scheme. As to the impact of the programme in alleviating poverty, only 18.75 per cent were able to cross the poverty line.

Out of them, only 23 households annual income was less than Rs. 400, 12 households had between Rs. 400-600 and 14 households had an annual income above Rs. 800. He also made a note that all the schemes were not equally remunerative. Many schemes were not capable of generating sufficient income because of limited market potential. The study also notes that the targets for employment creation under the IRDP are unrealistic. The observation of this study that the majority of the beneficiaries to the extent of 80 per cent (based on annual family income of less than Rs. 3,500) and 63.25 per cent (based on monthly per capita income of less than Rs. 76) for non-agricultural purposes, in case of non SC households the corresponding percentages are 40 and 60 respectively. The study further observes that while the income of the SC beneficiaries has increased by 15.64 per cent, the income of the non SC beneficiaries has increased by 22.16 per cent after being included in the IRDP. While in case of SC category the expenditure has increased by 15.38 per cent, in case of non SC category the increase is 22.11 per cent.

Panda[15] conducted a study on implementation of IRDP in Niali block of Cuttack district in Orissa. Data on annual income and expenditure of the sample households (50) for the year 1980-81 and 1982-83 (before and after the IRDP assistance) are collected. The study reveals that the sample beneficiaries under Scheduled Castes category have larger family size than that of the beneficiaries under non-Scheduled Caste category. The beneficiaries under non-Scheduled Caste category, have received much higher amount of assets than that of the beneficiaries under SC category. The subsidy component of the assistance forms a higher percentage in case of the beneficiaries under non-SC category than that of the SC category.

The study further reveals that 52 per cent of assistance provided for livestock and 48 per cent for non-agricultural purposes. While out of the total sample of SC households, 64 per cent have received assistance for livestock and 36 per cent for non-agricultural purposes, in case on non-SC households the corresponding percentages are 40 and 60 respectively. The study further observes that while the income of the SC beneficiaries has increased by 15.64 per cent, the income of the non-SC beneficiaries has increased by 22.16 per cent, after being included in IRDP. While in case of SC category the expenditure has increased by 15.38 per cent, in case of non-SC category the increase is 22.11 per cent.

NIRD conducted a study[16] of field level implementation of IRDP and other rural development projects in India by taking a sample of 193 beneficiaries and 109 non-beneficiaries in nine selected villages of Narasaraopet block in Guntur District of Andhra Pradesh. The focus of the study was to identify the constraints in IRDP implementation and to evaluate the success of it in terms of raising the beneficiaries above the poverty line. The major deficiencies observed by the study in implementation of IRDP are: *(a)* Adhoc selection of SC and ST beneficiaries, *(b)* difficulties and errors in computing *'net annual income'*, *(c)* asset-ownership orientation of bankers in financing schemes of IRDP, *(d)* frequent visits to bank office or *'suitable monetary incentive'* offers to the bankers by the applicants to get the work done quickly, *(e)* an alleged understanding between the seller and the *'purchase committee'* to inflate the price of the animal or input to accommodate the *'commission'* to the committee members. With regard to alleviation of poverty it was found that about 21 per cent of the beneficiaries of dairying scheme and 47 per cent of the rickshaw-pulling scheme had crossed the cutoff point. The study recommended structural reforms to separate the apparatus of regulating administration from that of development administration for better results.

Daljit Singh Dhillon in his state level study[17] examined the appropriateness of the beneficiaries selected under IRDP and the criteria laid down for their selection and various other aspects. Although majority of the assets created under the IRDP increased the income, only 53 per cent could cross the poverty line. In the case of 63 per cent beneficiaries the assets were found to be intact while in the remaining 37 per cent they were missing. Majority of the beneficiaries reported that the rate of interest charged was very high and some of the beneficiaries reported that they had to bribe the bank officials.

Balishter and Umesh Chandra[18] conducted a case study at Etah district in Uttar Pradesh. For assessing the impact of bank finance on family incomes of the beneficiary families and number of families crossing the poverty line, a sample of 150 beneficiary families were selected from 10 sample villages. Primary data for these families were collected for the year 1982-83 and 1984-85 (before and after bank finance). The main conclusions that emerged from this study are: (i) The weaker sections, including small and marginal farmers and landless labourers, comprise about 79 per cent of all families in the study area. (ii) The SC and ST families respectively comprise 33 and 67 per cent of the total poor families. (iii) The purchase of buffaloes and bullocks has been the dominant purpose of loans accounting for 76 per cent of the total beneficiary families as well as the amount of loans. (4) For small and marginal farmers the purchase of bullocks was the most dominant purpose accounting for over 43 per cent of the total loan while purchase of milch animals accounted for about 39 per cent of loan. In case of landless labourers, the purchase of milch animals was the most dominant purpose accounting for about 56 per cent of the total loan. (v) Impact of bank finance (regarding income generation) was relatively more on the landless labourers both in case of SC (49 per cent) and non-SC (48 per cent) beneficiaries. (vi) Non-agricultural activities have a higher income generating potential than agricultural activities. (vii) Out of 150 beneficiary families 99 or about 66 per cent were able to cross the poverty line of Rs. 3,500, of which 19 families were already above the poverty line before assistance. (viii) The large proportion of beneficiaries (44 per cent) who crossed poverty line were in higher income brackets (Rs. 3,000—3,500) before IRDP assistance. The study further reported that several problems which caused inadequate impact on income generation. These are delay in disbursal of loan, poor quality of assets, higher prices of assets charged by sellers, delay in releasing subsidy, bribe taken by implementing agencies, lack of supporting facilities, lack of guidance and insure cover.

K. Subba Rao[19] based on evaluation studies on the IRDP concluded that a particular household crosses the poverty line depending on *(a)* the initial income level of the household, *(b)* investment made on the household, *(c)* incremental income realised by the household and *(d)* sustained flow of income over a number of years, choice of the asset, capabilities of the household infrastructural support and demand for the output generated. So the index of crossing the poverty line is inappropriate for assessing the impact of the IRDP intervention, given sharp differences in the initial income level and the IRDP investments of selected households across the states. A very poor household may be expected to climb the income ladder only gradually, even with governmental support.

R.K. Mahajan is his micro level study[20] made an enquiry into the gains of the IRDP in terms of income and consumption and employment to different target groups. He has analysed that there is undue delay in providing assistance to the beneficiaries both at the block level and at the bank level. There is corruption particularly for clearance of schemes from the DRDA. There is no follow-up action for the old beneficiaries. Marketing facilities for the products generated by the assets sponsored by the IRDP is very poor and the recovery of loan is also poor.

P.S.N. Tiwari[21] was undertaken a study with the objectives (i) to examine the awareness of the recipients of IRDP as regards to various schemes of rural development and (ii) to assess the impact of IRDP on the people who are below poverty line. A sample of 65 recipients and 15 officials were selected from the villages of Uttar Pradesh. Data were collected through interview schedules. The study founds that, out of the five heads under which IRDP provides loans, all the recipients were aware of the provision of loan for animal husbandry. About 89.2 per cent showed their awareness of loan provisions for promoting business, 38.5 per cent for irrigation, 44.6 per cent for agriculture and 61.5 per cent for cottage industry. Gram Pradhan, block personnel, friends, etc., constituted the sources of information for these recipients. As regards the selection of beneficiaries it was observed that about 71 per cent of the respondents received benefits who were not entitled for the benefits under the scheme.

About 87.7 per cent beneficiaries reported that the selection of beneficiaries was not according to the set procedures. With regard to the loan amount it was observed that only 23 per cent of the respondents received the exact amount of loan sanctioned to them. Moreover, they had to pay 15 per cent of the sanctioned loan to the officers and other personnel as bribe.

K.M. George[22] examined the impact of the IRDP implementation in two blocks of Alwar district of Rajasthan. It was conducted in a sample of 20 per cent selected through multi-stage sampling technique out of the 400 beneficiaries. The major schemes covered in the study were dairying, camel cart and sheep-rearing.

The data shows that the total income realised by all the beneficiaries from all sources was Rs. 99,698 before introduction of IRDP but it rose to Rs. 1,49,151 after IRDP. Income from agricultural labour worked out to 55.07 per cent of the total income before IRDP, it was 36.81 per cent of the total income after IRDP. Dairying contributed 36.58 per cent of the total income after the implementation of IRDP whereas it was 5.12 per cent before IRDP. The average employment generated per beneficiary household was to the extent of 125.22 mandays after the implementation of IRDP. About 40 per cent of the beneficiaries were regular in repayment of the loans. Lack of veterinary facilities, high mortality rate of sheep and lambs and inadequate marketing facilities were some of the reasons identified for poor recovery.

Jasbir Singh and Deb's[23] study aims at assessing the social and economic impact of IRDP. The study was conducted in 12 villages in two districts of Punjab. The total sample for this study was 396 households. The study observed that financial assistance from banks was also one of the most important elements in improving the socio-economic conditions of the people. The family income of all categories of respondents in highly developed district was higher than that of their counterparts in less developed district. The average per capita income of all the occupational categories in developed district was higher than that of the less developed district. Again, the per capita income of the beneficiaries was more than that of the non-beneficiaries in both the districts. The study further observes that the per household net income of the non-SC category has increased by Rs. 30.47 and that of SC category by Rs. 3.58, during a year after the commencement of IRDP. The study concludes that for the effective implementation of the programme, only providing different assets to the beneficiaries is not enough; afterwards follow-up action is needed to see that the assets become a growing income generating proposition to the beneficiary households in future.

Ghosh[24] conducted a study with a view to assessing the awareness level of IRDP beneficiaries and evolving suitable strategy for enhancing their awareness level. The study was conducted through field work in the three blocks of Nadia District in West Bengal during June to August, 1990. A total of 180 beneficiaries assisted in the task during the year 1988-89 spanning over 18 villages in the selected blocks. The study reveals that regarding the objective of the programme, 58.33 per cent beneficiaries responded that it was aimed at generating self-employment, while 61.11 per cent replied that the objective was income generation.

C.H. Pothuluru's[25] study is confined to Mothkur Mandal located in the district of Nalgonda in Andhra Pradesh. The study is based on primary data collected through field survey from 120 household beneficiaries. The objectives of the study are: to find out the proportion of beneficiary households which have retained and diverted the assets/financial assistance and to study the recovery performance in various schemes of the programme. The study revealed that (i) a considerable amount of investment given under IRDP, has been diverted to household consumption (39.4 per cent), followed by repayment of old debt (23.6 per cent), marriages (21.3 per cent), and the remaining portion for acquiring the income yielding assets of their own choice (15.7 per cent), (ii) 30 per cent of the beneficiaries repaid the entire amount of investment while 60 per cent of them have repaid partially. The rest of the wilful defaulters, who have not paid a single pie even after the lapse of three or four years. The beneficiaries under the tailoring scheme stand first in repayment (66.66 per cent), followed by handloom weavers (56 per cent), sheep rearing (25 per cent) and new well sinking (5.1 per cent).

The objectives of the A.M. Jose's[26] study were: to examine the extent of women's participation in rural development activities and to assess the impact of IRDP on women's economic status vis-a-vis their household economic status. Two blocks, namely, Panthalayani, a developed block from Kazhikode District and Mananthavady, a less developed block from Wynad District in Kerala were selected for the study. The study revealed that the women work for more number of days in Mananthavady block when compared to Panthalayani block. The contribution of women to the total household income was found to be much less in both the blocks in comparison with their share of employment. Women in beneficiary households were found to have contributed higher share of income and had higher employment than the women in non-beneficiary households.

Balaramulu, Ch.,[27] has attempted to find out the impact of IRDP in Nalgonda District of Andhra Pradesh. He has undertaken the study of 547 households which were covered by DRDA during 1980-81 to 1982-83 in the year 1986-87 in 18 villages. In his findings, out of 63 households in agricultural schemes which retained the assets, only 6.4 per cent have crossed the poverty line. Out of 7 households which retained the assets in animal husbandry scheme, there is a negative income of Rs. 19.70. And among 76 households, which were given schemes in minor irrigation, 8 per cent could cross the poverty line. The study reveals that considerable percentage (40 per cent) of beneficiaries retained the asset and continue to derive the benefits out of these assets with the regional variations. It is interesting to note that only little more than 14 per cent of the beneficiaries in the developed block, more than half of the beneficiaries in less developed block and an overwhelming percentage (81.5 per cent) of beneficiaries in medium developed block have retained their assets. It is to be noted that the IRD Programmes are highly successful in less developed areas than in developed areas. The study further reveals that the large percentage of forward cases (63 per cent) and STs (54 per cent) are retaining the asset whereas backward classes and SCs are mainly diverting them. The nature of scheme/asset which they have received is one of the causes for such behaviour.

The Department of Economics, University of Cochin, conducted[28] an evaluation of IRDP in Kottayam District of Kerala. The study covered 300 beneficiaries belonging to 1981-82 and 1982-83. The main objectives of the study were to assess the impact of the programme and to find out the shortcomings. The study revealed that income had increased in the case of 55 per cent of the beneficiaries whereas 39 per cent crossed the poverty line. About 63 per cent of the beneficiaries reported that the scheme had created additional employment. As this percentage is slightly higher (8 per cent) compared to those who recorded an increase in their incomes, it follows that, increase in employment need not always accompany increase in income, as it is generally believed. A wide range of increase in their annual income varying from Rs. 200 to Rs. 2,500 was reported by the beneficiaries was as high as 40 per cent. The study recommended for active involvement of target groups in implementation of the programme by constituting selection committees and follow-up committees.

The study under review was a case study[29] on impact of IRDP on agricultural labourers in two blocks of Kolar District of Karnataka. Out of the total of 150 beneficiaries for the years 1983 and 1984, 70 were rural agricultural labourers were taken for the case study. The study analysed the factors like the scheme provided, quantum of assistance given, income and employment generated, loan repayment and the number of beneficiaries crossing the poverty line. The study reveals that 99 per cent of schemes constitute agriculture and allied activities and one per cent of ISB sector. The quantum of assistance provided in animal husbandry and agricultural schemes are below the normal of Rs. 3,000. A larger number of beneficiaries from animal husbandry scheme have moved to higher income slabs than the beneficiaries from agricultural scheme. The repayment performance of the beneficiaries of the animal husbandry scheme is the highest followed by those of the agricultural scheme, at it was the lowest in the ISB scheme. The study further reveals that 24 per cent of the beneficiaries have crossed the poverty line. The majority of the beneficiaries who crossed the poverty line were all from animal husbandry and only one beneficiary from the ISB sector. None crossed the poverty line who took up schemes under agriculture.

The Planning Evaluation Organisation (PEO)[30] conducted an all India level survey in 1985 and reported that nearly 26 per cent of the selected beneficiaries were already above the poverty line (Rs. 3,500/-). Only 29 per cent of the target families were selected in the meeting of grama sabha and the remaining 71 per cent by the block level officials. Nearly 49.4 per cent of the selected beneficiaries crossed the poverty line. The majority of the beneficiaries in the lowest income group were not able to cross the poverty line due to inadequate assistance and partly because of other factors. The problem of lack of coordination at the district level was also experienced. Absence of a strong administrative set up, lack of proper administrative control of project officers over B.D.Os, lack of training facilities etc., were also noticed.

The Reserve Bank of India[31] conducted a study on the IRDP at an all-India level and analysed that no household survey was done for the identification of the beneficiaries. The percentage of ineligible beneficiaries who received the assistance was more. The study also reported that there was insistence on additional security by banks contrary to the government instructions and delay in the disposal of loan applications and there was also lack of coordination between the DRDA and block level officials.

The National Bank of Agriculture and Rural Development (NABARD) conducted a study[32] at an India level on the IRDP and pointed out that 47 per cent of the eligible beneficiaries increased their income above the poverty line. The programme pushed up the average income of the beneficiaries by 22 per cent from Rs. 1,967/- to Rs. 585/-.

The proportion was relatively high in Punjab, West Bengal, Haryana, Uttar Pradesh and Maharashtra, modest in Orissa, Gujarat and Madhya Pradesh and low in Kerala, Karnataka, Assam, Bihar, Tamilnadu, Rajasthan and Andhra Pradesh. The Selection of non-eligible families who got assistance under the programme was to the extent of 15 per cent.

The State Bank of India conducted evaluation studies[33] at the district level and concluded that there was wrong identification of the beneficiaries and no meeting of the grama sabha was convened for confirming the identification of the IRDP beneficiaries. The study also reported that the IRDP generated additional employment and income and increased the consumption level. It further revealed that about 39 per cent of the beneficiaries crossed the poverty line.

The following conclusions emerged from the review of various studies presented above:

1. The studies revealed that there are wide range of variations in the estimated number of persons crossing the poverty line. It varies from 6.40 per cent to 81.0 per cent of the assisted families;
2. It was found that a proper administrative arrangements were lacking for the execution of the programme. In many districts block perspective plans were not prepared according to the guidelines largely because of lack of technical personnel and commitment on the part of official machinery;
3. It was also observed that in several cases the identification of beneficiary households was wrong. Consequently a good number of ineligible families grabbed the benefits;
4. Several studies revealed that the quantum of assistance given to the beneficiaries was not adequate to generate incremental income to enable them to cross the poverty line;
5. The non-percolation effect of assistance as mentioned in several studies, is due to several factors the important being (i) leakages in the loans and subsidies, (ii) misuse

of loans, and (iii) lack of training to put the assets to the best use;

6. Delays in providing financial assistance and unrealistic payment schedules have been responsible for unsatisfactory loan repayment performance. There are also cases of wilful default due to sale of assets, utilisation of loans for purposes other than those for which they are granted. It was also found that on account of deficiencies in administration, the non-poor were able to grab loans by getting them identified as poor or using poor-persons for acquiring assets by paying them nominal amounts;

7. It was found that targets were fixed without understanding the magnitude of poverty and resource availability in a particular region. Beneficiary schemes were also formulated without taking into account the resource endowment of a particular region.

On account of various defects in preparation and implementation of the schemes the benefits are being liberally passed on to the well-off sections and irrigated and agriculturally prosperous regions with the result that with growth the roots of inequalities are getting stronger in village economies.

REFERENCES

1. Paul Samuel, *"Strategic Management of Development Programmes, Guidelines for Action"*, International Labour Office, Geneva, 1983.
2. D. Bandyopadhyay, *'IRDP—A Programme for Income Generation through Asset Endowment and Skill Formation'*, edited by Rizwal Islam in the book, *'Strategies for Alleviating Poverty in Rural Asia'*, ILO Publication, Bangalore, 1985.
3. M.L. Dantwala, *'Reconciling with Social Justice' in Agrarian Structure and Poverty*, p. 51 and *'IRDP and Village Structure,* Economic and Political Weekly, Vol. XXII, No. 22, May, 30, 1987.
4. N. Rath, *'Garibi Hatao-Can IRDP do it?'* Economic and Political Weekly, Vol. XX, No. 13, March 30, 1985, p. 561.
5. Institute for Financial Management and Research, *An Economic Assessment of Poverty Eradication and Rural Unemployment Programmes and their Prospects (Mimeograph), Madras, 1985.*

6. Robert V. Pulley, *Making the Poor Credit Worthy*. A case study of IRDP in India, World Bank, Washington, USA, 1989, p. 47.

7. R.N. Tripathi and others, *IRDP in South India: An Evaluation*, National Institute of Rural Development, Hyderabad, 1995.

8. B.C. Muthayya *et. al. Receptivity and Reaction to IRDP—A Study in Three States'*, Journal of Rural Development, 2 (3) pp. 318-350, 1983.

9. State Bank of India (1985-86). *"Integrated Rural Development Programme: An Impact Evaluation"*. State Bank of India Monthly Review, Vol. XXVI, No. 8, August, 1987, p. 371-402.

10. N.J. Korien, *IRDP—How Relevant Is It*, Economic Political Weekly, Vol, XXII, No. 52, December 26th, 1987.

11. Government of India, Department of Rural Development, *Concurrent Evaluation of IRDP*, The Main Findings of the Survey for January-December, 1987, New Delhi, 1988.

12. Indira, Hirway, *'Critique of target group approach: A study of Gujarat.'* Indian Journal of Economics, Vol. XXXIV, No. 3, July/September, 1984, pp. 289-297.

13. Naidu, V.J. and K. Chandrasekhara Rao, *'Income and Employment Generation under IRDP: A Case Study of Guntur District'*, proceedings of the Sixth Annual Conference of Andhra Pradesh Economic Association held at Satavahana Institute of P.G. Studies, Karimnagar on 23-24 January, 1988, pp. 19-26.

14. Kutty Krishnan, A.C., *"A Case Study of Integrated Rural Development Programme in Kerala Village"*. Indian Journal of Agricultural Economics, Vol. XXXIX, No. 3, July—September, 1984, pp. 259-265.

15. R.K. Panda, *"Implementation of IRDP in Orissa,"* Kurukshetra, Vol. XXXIII, No. 11, August, 1985, pp. 26-28.

16. National Institute of Rural Development, *Case Study on Field Level Implementation of Rural Development Programmes with Special Reference to IRDP (Hyderabad, NIRD, 1983).*

17. Daljit Singh Dhillon, *'Integrated Rural Development*: Vohra Publishers and Distributors, Allahabad, 1991, pp. 96-97.

18. Dr. Balishter and R. Umesh Chandra, *'Integrated Rural Development Programme—A Study in Eath District of Uttar Pradesh,"* Yojana, Vol. 34, No. 6, April 1—15, 1990, pp. 25–27.

19. K.Subba Rao, *'Regional Variations, in the Impact of Anti-poverty Programmes—A Review of Evidence,'* Economic and Political Weekly, Vol. No. 43, October, 26, 1985, p. 1829.

20. R.K. Mahajan *'Differential Gains of IRDP—A Micro Level Study.* Concept Publishing Company, New Delhi, 1991, pp. 97-167.

21. Tiwari, P.S.N., *"Goals and Achievement of IRDP: An Assessment,"* Indian Journal of Community Guidance Service 5 (31) September, 1988, pp. 85-86.

22. George, K.M., *"Rural Development Programme: It's Strength and Weaknesses, Rajasthan,"* Indian Journal of Agricultural Economics, 39 (3) July-September, 1984, pp. 266-275.

23. Jasbir K. Singh and D.C. Deb, *"Socio-economic Impact of IRDP in Punjab"*, Kurukshetra, Vol. XXXIII, No. 11, August, 1985, pp. 29-32.

24. Dr. Ghosh, D.H., *"Awareness of IRDP Beneficiaries: A Study"*, Kurukshetra, 39 (12) September, 1991, pp. 15-19.

25. Pothuluru, C.H., *"Recovery of Financial Assistance Under IRDP"*, Kurukshetra, Vol. XXXIX, No. 6, March, 1991, pp. 27-31.

26. Jose, A.M., *"IRDP and Employment Generation for Women: A Micro-level Study in Kerala"*. Man and Development, 11 (2), June, 1989, pp. 35-53.

27. Balaramulu, Ch., *"Evaluation of IRDP in Nalgonda District of Andhra Pradesh: A Case Study of a Public Policy,"* Centre for Economic and Social Studies, Begumpet, Hyderabad, 1988.

28. Department of Applied Economics, *Integrated Rural Development—Evaluation and Impact Study*. Cochin University, Cohin, 1984, Mimes.

29. Thippaiah, P. and M. Devendra Babu, *"Impact of IRDP on Agricultural Labourers: A Case Study,"* Kurukshetra, Vol. XXXVIII, No. 9, June, 1990, pp. 28-31.

30. Planning Commission. *'Planning Evaluation Organisation Study—Confined to 16 States, 33 Districts, 66 Blocks and 1,170 Households,'* 1985.

31. Reserve Bank of India, *An Evaluation of IRDP in India*, 1984.

32. NABARD, *"Evaluation of IRDP at All India Level,"* Bombay, 1987.

33. State Bank of India, *'A Study on IRDP in 10 Lead Districts in India,'* 1984.

I.R.D.P. in Anantapur District

Profile of Anantapur District

Anantapur district was part of Bellary district in the year of 1880 and was separated from the district in the year of 1882. It was expanded with the addition of Kadiri taluk from Cuddapah district in the year 1910 and Rayadurg taluk from Bellary district in the year 1956. At present the district has been divided into three revenue divisions namely Anantapur Division, Dharmavaram Division and Penukonda Division. The three revenue divisions consists of 962 villages, 63 revenue mandals. Anantapur division has 20 mandals, Dharmavaram Division has 17 mandals and Penukonda division has 26 mandals.

Boundary and Topography

Anantapur district lies between '13°–40′ and 15°–15′ northern latitude and 76°–50′ and 78°–30′ eastern longitude. It is bounded by Bellary and Kurnool districts on the north, Cuddapah district on the east, Kolar district of Karnataka state on the south, Chittoor district on the south and Chitradurga district of Karnataka state on the south-west.

The following Table—4.1 shows the catchment areas of the five major rivers in Anantapur district with their ayacut area.

Table—4.1

Catchment Areas of Major Rivers and Drainage Densities

Sl. No.	*Major Rivers*	*Catchment area in km²*	*Percentage of the total geographical area of the district*	*Drainage density in km²*
1.	Pennar	8,869	46.4	0.45
2.	Chitravathi	6,026	31.5	0.35
3.	Hagari	2,354	12.3	0.71
4.	Papagni	1,187	6.2	0.32
5.	Swarnamukhi	689	3.6	0.47

Source : Handbook of Statistics, 1993-94, p. 35.

Rivers

The district is not endowed with perennial rivers. Seasonal rivers like Pennar, Jayamangala, Chitravathi, Vedavathi and Hagari rivers flow during the rainy days and benefit the seasonal requirements of the farmers on river banks in 317 kms. route of the rivers, streams like Kushavathi in Hindupur, Swarnamukhi in Madakasira, Thadakaleru and Pandameru in Anantapur mandal. Maddileru in Kadiri mandal and Papagni in Thanakal mandal are the important water supply sources to various large and medium irrigation tanks in the district.

Forest Resources

The district is very poor in forest wealth both in terms of area and richness of flora. 4.86 lakh acres constituting 10.3 per cent of the total geographical area is classified as forests against optimal area of 33 per cent indicated the national forest policy The value of forest produce such as beedi leaves, custard apples, tamarind and soapnut is meager and other resource is agave (Sisil) a plant which has a wild growth from which fiber is being extracted. The forest in Anantapur district means only wild bushes and rocky terrain.

Rainfall and Climate

Anantapur district is most driest part of the country with the second lowest average rainfall of 520.4 mm after Jaisalmar district in the State of Rajasthan and is classified as tropical arid with an aridity index of 72.5 and the rainfall is highly erratic. Normally south-west monsoon favours with the 60 per cent of the total rainfall (310.8 mm) and being far away from East Coast. North-east monsoon will not be vigorous in the district (147 mm). Intermittent dry spell ranging from 4 to 6 weeks in the crucial state of crops growth period. Coupled with velocity winds often result in low productivity of crops. The altitude varies from 990′ above MSL at Tadipatri to 2000′ above Mean Sea level in Madakasira mandal. Maximum temperature ranging between 20.1°C to 38.4°C recorded during the months of March, April and May. November to January are the cooler months with a minimum temperature of 17.2°C.

Soils

The soils in Anantapur district are predominantly red, except, Kanekal, Bommanahal, Vidapanakal, Uravakonda, Vajrakarur, Guntakal, Gooty, Pamidi, Peddavadugur, Yadiki, Tadipatri, Yellanur, Pedda Pappur and Putlur. In these mandals red and black soils occupy almost in equal proportions. In the whole district 76 per cent are red soil, 24 per cent are black soils.

Population

The district has population of 31.81 lakhs as per 1991 census accounting for 4 per cent of the State's population. The decimal growth rate in 1981 is 24.93 per cent slightly higher than State average. The density of population is 172 per sq. km. in the district as against 242 per sq. km. of the State. The literate population constitute 11.14 lakhs of the total population compared to State population of 244.88 lakhs. 77 per cent of the population lives in villages. Scheduled Castes population constitutes 14.19 per cent, Scheduled Tribes about 3.49 per cent and minority communities about 12 per cent. The work force in the district constitutes about 46.02 per cent of the population of 32.20 per cent are its agricultural sector. There are 496 females per 1000 males. Comparative population statistics of Anantapur district is shown in Table—4.2.

Table—4.2
Comparative Population Statistics of Anantapur District

(in Lakhs)

Sl. No.	*Item*	*1961*	*1971*	*1981*	*1991*
1.	Population	17.68	21.15	26.18	31.84
2.	Females	8.59 (48.59)	10.29 (48.65)	12.65 (48.31)	15.62 (48.62)
3.	Males	9.09 (51.41)	10.86 (51.35)	13.53 (51.69)	16.36 (51.38)
4.	Rural Population	14.60 (82.57)	17.39 (82.22)	20.88 (79.76)	24.37 (76.54)
5.	Urban Population	3.08 (17.43)	3.76 (17.78)	5.30 (20.24)	7.47 (23.46)
6.	Literates	3.64 (20.58)	3.04 (14.37)	7.09 (27.08)	11.36 (35.68)
7.	Workers	9.01 (50.96)	9.09 (46.80)	11.06 (42.24)	13.60 (42.71)
8.	Non-Workers	8.67 (49.04)	11.25 (53.20)	15.12 (57.76)	18.24 (57.29)
9.	Cultivators	4.43 (25.05)	3.27 (15.46)	4.52 (17.27)	4.74 (14.89)
10	Agricultural Labourers	2.37 (13.40)	3.46 (16.36)	3.82 (14.59)	5.57 (17.49)
11.	Scheduled Caste	2.36 (13.34)	2.78 (13.14)	3.49 (13.33)	4.42 (13.89)
12.	Scheduled Tribe	0.49 (2.77)	0.65 (3.07)	0.82 (3.13)	1.19 (3.73)
13.	Density of Population (per Sq. Km)	92	111	137	166

Sources: 1. Census Reports of India 1961, 1971, 1981, Govt. of India, New Delhi.

2. Census of India, 1991, Andhra Pradesh, Series—2, Paper I of 1991, Director of Census Operations, Andhra Pradesh, Hyderabad.

Note : Figures in parentheses shows their percentage to total population.

Land Utilisation

The total geographical area of the district is 47.28 lakh acres. The land utilisation pattern as available in the district during the year 1996-97 shows that the net area sown is 10,62,755 hectares which form 55.5 per cent of the area. The total cropped area is 10,63,160 hectares.

The cultivated area of the district is 10,63,160 hectares and of which 9,21,394 hectares is under Kharif and 1,41,766 hectares is under Rabi season during the year 1996-97. The district occupies the lowest position in respect of irrigation facilities. Out of the gross irrigated area of 1,84,050 hectares during the 1996-97 canals accounted for 17.34 per cent, tanks 11.84 per cent, wells 68.29 per cent and other sources 1.00 per cent all the principal sources except canals are non-precarious.

MINERAL RESOURCES

Anantapur Resources

Anantapur district is rich in mineral resources and is well-known for gold and diamond deposits. The main mineral deposits are limestone, barites, dolomite, iron ore, korandum, steatite, white shale, serpentine and green quartz available in the Anantapur district. Tadipatri is rich in cement grade limestone deposits.

Place of Tourist Importance

Anantapur district is also a tourist place. Gugudu is the village in Narpala Mandal which is known for its Moharram festival and Sri Kullayswamy temple. Lepakshi of Hindupur mandal is popular for its Veerabhadra temple and the huge stone Nandi stands nearby. The temple has a veritable treasure of sculpture and architecture. Pilgrims visit the place mostly for Sivarathri.

Penna Ahobilam is famous for its temple of Sri Lakshmi Narasimha Swamy the temple of Lakshmi, the Lord consort is situated by the side of main shrines. There is a spring channel in the temple known as Bugga Koneru.

Puttaparti is situated on the banks of Chitravathi in Puttaparthi mandal, which is universally famous with the abode of Sri Sathya Saibaba who is credited with occult powers. Super Speciality Hospital also located where free treatment is given to one and all which is famous all over the world.

Likewise, Penakacherla dam is also a site seeing place, Kasapuram, Aluru Kona and Gorantla, Hemavathi are also of important tourist attractions because of the temples situated in these areas. The Gutibayalu is about 25 km south-east of Kadiri has world famous Banyan tree covering 2.02 hectares of land.

Education

The district has good number of educational institutions to cater the educational needs of the people. It can be seen from the table that colleges imparting general education are out numbering technical institutions in the district. The particulars of these institutions furnished in Table—4.3.

Table—4.3

Educational Institutions in Anantapur District

Sl. No.	*Name of the Educational Institution*	*No. of Educational Institutions*
1.	Primary Schools	2,771
2.	Upper Primary Schools	283
3.	Secondary Schools	295
4.	High Schools attached to Junior Colleges	12
5.	Junior Colleges	71
6.	Degree Colleges	20
7.	Universities	2
8.	Engineering College	1
9.	Polytechnic Colleges	2
10.	Industrial Training Institutes	6
11.	B.Ed. College	1

Source : Handbook of Statistics, Anantapur 1997-98.

On the basis of the facts presented in the table it is clear that Anantapur district provides everything like land, water, power, finance and labour for the enterprises the district has got good transport facilities.

I.R.D.P. Beneficiaries in Anantapur District

An attempt is made in this chapter to analyse the socio-economic, working conditions, literacy, family income of the beneficiaries.

A sample of 100 respondents were interviewed for evaluating the impact of IRDP in the study area.

Housing Conditions of the Beneficiaries

A house can be defined in many ways. The official definition of a house could be described as a structure with walls on four sides, a roof on top and an opening in the front and it is a residential abode of an individual where he lives with his family.

Lack of shelter or its degradation is an inseparable part of poverty. The houses in which the beneficiaries has been classified into three categories i.e., (i) pucca, (ii) semi-pucca, (iii) kutcha.

The possession of a town house, or rented house, whether it is a pucca house, semi-pucca or kutcha houses by the beneficiaries, also have an impact on the programme.

Table—4.4 gives a picture about the position and the possession of the house by the beneficiaries. Out of the total beneficiaries 59 per cent have pucca houses, 20 per cent have semi-pucca and 21 per cent have Kutcha houses. Out of 33 Scheduled Caste beneficiaries, 52.38 per cent have kutcha houses and 37.29 per cent have pucca houses. Scheduled Tribes have only 14.29 per cent kutcha houses. Out of 47 backward caste beneficiaries, 45.76 per cent have pucca houses, 65 per cent have semi-pucca houses and 33.33 per cent have kutcha houses, among the other castes 16.94 per cent have pucca houses, 35 per cent have semi-pucca houses.

Table—4.4
Caste-wise Housing Conditions of the Selected Beneficiaries in Anantapur Rural Mandal

Sl. No.	Type of House	Caste-wise				Total
		SCs	STs	BCs	OCs	
1.	Pucca	22 (37.29)	–	27 (45.76)	10 (16.94)	59 (59.00)
2.	Semi-pucca	–	–	13 (65.00)	7 (35.00)	20 (20.00)
3.	Kutcha	11 (52.38)	3 (14.29)	7 (33.33)	– –	21 (21.00)
	Total	**33**	**3**	**47**	**17**	**100**

Note : Figures in parenthesis indicate percentage of total.
Source : Computed from the primary data.

Size of the Family

At the very outset, it is worthwhile to study the size of the families of the beneficiaries. It is the most needed characteristic to satisfy the aspects of the study namely impact on income and employment generation. The family size of the beneficiaries is shown in Table—4.5.

Table—4.5
Family Size of the Selected Beneficiaries

Sl. No.	Target	Size of the family		Total
		1—4	5—9	
1.	Small Farmers	4 (20)	16 (80)	20 (100)
2.	Marginal Farmers	6 (30)	14 (70)	20 (100)
3.	Agricultural Labourers	9 (45)	11 (55)	20 (100)
4.	Non-agricultural Labourers	8 (40)	12 (60)	20 (100)
5.	Rural Artisans	11 (55)	9 (45)	20 (100)
	Total	**38**	**62**	**100**

Note : Figures in the parenthesis denote percentage.
Source : Computed from the primary data.

Table—4.5 shows that majority of the beneficiary families have the size of more than five members i.e., 62 per cent of beneficiaries are found in the family size of 5-9. In all the target groups, the percentage of beneficiary families is high in the family size of 5-9 compared to the family of 1-4.

Age-wise Distribution

Age-wise distribution of the members in the beneficiary households is shown in the Table—4.6. Proper implementation of the programmes mainly depends on the working age group of the population. So, it is necessary to study age-wise distribution of the sample households. People belong to the age group of 26 and above years are considered as working labour force.

Table—4.6

Age-wise Distribution of the Selected IRDP Beneficiaries

Sl. No.	*Target Groups*	*Beneficiaries age (in years)*		*Total*
		0—25	*26 above*	
1.	Small Farmers	6 (30)	14 (70)	20 (100)
2.	Marginal Farmers	5 (25)	15 (75)	20 (100)
3.	Agricultural Labourers	1 (5)	19 (95)	20 (100)
4.	Non-agricultural Labourers	3 (15)	17 (85)	20 (100)
5.	Rural Artisans	8 (40)	12 (60)	20 (100)
	Total	**23**	**67**	**100**

Note : Figures in the parenthesis denote percentage.
Source : Computed from primary data.

It is found the Table—4.6 that the working age group (i.e., above 26 years age) people is more at 57 per cent. Irrespective of the target group 23.00 per cent of beneficiaries fall in the age-wise group of below 25 years. Under the small farmers, the working labour force accounts to 70.00 per cent. Under marginal farmers group, the working labour force is 75.00 per cent. Among agricultural labourers, the working labour force accounts to 95.00 per cent of beneficiaries i.e., age group of above 26 years.

Literacy Level

Table 4.7 shows the literacy level of the beneficiary households, which represents one of the important social characteristics of the population.

Table—4.7
Literacy Level of the Selected IRDP Beneficiaries

Sl. No.	*Target Groups*	*Literacy Level*		*Total*
		Total Illiterates	*Total Literates*	
1.	Small Farmers	8 (40)	12 (60)	20 (100)
2.	Marginal Farmers	3 (15)	17 (85)	20 (100)
3.	Agricultural Labourers	2 (10)	18 (90)	20 (100)
4.	Non-agricultural Labourers	9 (45)	11 (55)	20 (120)
5.	Rural Artisans	7 (35)	13 (65)	20 (100)
	Total	**29**	**71**	**100**

Notice : Figures in the parenthesis denote percentage.
Source : Computed from primary data.

The Table—4.7 depicts that the illiterates are greater in the case of beneficiary households irrespective of the target group. The percentage of total illiterates accounts to 29 per cent. In the small farmers group, literates constitute 60 per cent and it is 85 per cent in the case of marginal farmers group. The agriculture labourers the percentage of literate accounts to 90 per cent in the case of non-agriculture labourers 55 per cent. Among the rural artisan labourers, the percentage of literates accounts to 65 per cent are among beneficiary households. In general, the literacy level is medium in the case of beneficiary households.

Caste-wise Distribution

The people consist of different caste groups since each caste has its own socio-economic and cultural background. Therefore, it is essential to distinguish the various caste dimensions considered in the study. The respondents for the study are selected from the following caste groups (i) Backward Castes (B.C.), (ii) Scheduled Castes (S.C.), (iii) Scheduled Tribes, (S.T.), and (iv) Other Caste (O.C.).

Table—4.8 clearly shows the caste-wise distribution of beneficiaries. It is evident from the Table—4.8 that irrespective of the target groups of beneficiaries, the Backward Caste

Table—4.8
Caste-Wise Distribution of Selected Beneficiaries

Sl. No.	*Target Groups*	*Caste-wise*				*Total*
		SCs	*STs*	*BCs*	*OCs*	
1.	Small Farmers	3 (15)	–	12 (60)	5 (25)	20 (100)
2.	Marginal Farmers	9 (45)	–	9 (45)	2 (10)	20 (100)
3.	Agricultural Labourers	12 (60)	–	5 (25)	3 (15)	20 (100)
4.	Non-Agricultural Labourers	7 (35)	–	7 (35)	6 (30)	20 (100)
5.	Rural Artisans	5 (25)	3 (15)	11 (55)	1 (5)	20 (100)
	Total	36	3	44	17	100

Note : Figures in brackets indicate percentage of total.
Source : Computed from the primary data.

households constitute 44 per cent. Irrespective of target groups, the Scheduled Caste families constitute 36 per cent. The Scheduled Tribes constitute 3 per cent whereas it is 17 per cent in the other caste group. The percentage of Scheduled Tribe beneficiaries is low since the percentage of Scheduled Tribes population is also low in the district. Hence, it is understood that top priority is given for the Backward Caste and Scheduled Caste under IRDP in the study area.

Size of the Operational Holdings

The size of the operational holdings of the beneficiaries is presented in Table—4.9. For the analysis of operation of holdings, only two sections of the target groups are taken into account i.e., small farmers and marginal farmers. The agricultural labourers are not taken into account since they are landless labourers.

Table—4.9
Size of the Operational Holdings of the Selected Beneficiaries

Sl. No.	*Target Groups*	*Average land (in acres)*		*Total*
		Wet	*Dry*	
1.	Small Farmers	0.60	4.05	4.11
2.	Marginal Farmers	0.20	2.00	2.20
	Total	**0.80**	**6.05**	**6.31**

Source : Computed from the primary data.

The Table—4.9 illustrates that the total average landholdings is greater in the case of small farmers. The total average landholding is 2.20 per cent for marginal farmers. The small farmers category, the average wet land holdings of the beneficiary is 0.60 acres, and in the case of dry land holdings, the beneficiaries have 4.05 acres. Among the marginal farmers, the beneficiaries have 0.20 acres of wet land and in the case of dry land holdings, the beneficiaries have 2.0 acres on an average.

Bank-wise Distribution of Financial Assistance

The bank-wise distribution of financial assistance under IRDP during 1997-98 is clearly shown in Table—4.10. Various banks have played their respective role in assisting the rural poor under IRDP in Anantapur Mandal.

Table—4.10
Bank-wise Financial Assistance under IRDP During 1997-98

Sl. No.	*Name of the Bank*	*Amount of loan provided*		*No. of beneficiaries Assisted*	
		Assistance given (in Rs.)	*Percentage to total*	*No. of Beneficiaries*	*Percentage to total*
1.	Syndicate Bank	5,36,870	44.99	82	51.90
2.	State Bank of India	4,16,571	34.91	44	27.85
3.	Andhra Bank	1,74,686	14.64	27	17.09
4.	Canara Bank	44,350	3.72	3	1.90
5.	SC Corporation	6,000	0.50	1	0.63
6.	ADCCB	14,850	1.24	1	0.63
	Total	**11,93,327**	**100.00**	**158**	**100.00**

Source : Data collected from the different banks of the Anantapur Mandal, Anantapur.

In Anantapur Mandal, there are 6 financial institutions which have distributed the credit during 1997-98.

Regarding the bank-wise performance of financial assistance for rural poor under IRDP in the mandal, it is found that Syndicate Bank occupies the first place by providing credit facilities for 51.90 per cent of beneficiaries during 1997-98. State Bank of India occupies the second place by providing credit facilities to 27.85 per cent of the rural poor. Andhra Bank occupies the third place by providing financial assistance to 17.09 per cent of the rural poor. The role played by the remaining banks in assisting the rural poor is almost negligible. Canara Bank assisted only 1.90 per cent of the total number of beneficiaries.

The role played by the Syndicate Bank in assisting to rural poor in the mandal is appreciable. The role of State Bank in providing financial assistance to the rural poor is also appreciable. These banks have played a crucial role in assisting the rural poor under IRDP. The Canara Bank played only a limited role in helping the rural poor and their performance is almost negligible in the mandal during 1997-98.

Programme-wise Performance of IRDP in Anantapur Mandal During 1996-97 to 1997-98

Scheme-wise progress and achievements of IRDP in Anantapur district has not been available in a detailed manner. Its performance in the mandal was available only from the year 1996-97 onwards. The table—4.11 shows the performance of IRDP during 1996-97 to 1997-98.

Table—4.11
Programme-wise Performance of IRDP in Anantapur Mandal During 1996-97 to 1997-98

Sl. No.	*Programmes*	*1996-97*		*1997-98*	
		No. of beneficiaries benefited	*Assistance given (in lakhs)*	*No. of beneficiaries benefited*	*Assistance given (in lakhs)*
1.	Tertiary/ ISB	17 (20)	1.45	103 (65.1)	4.98
2.	Sericulture	35 (41.2)	7.58	29 (18.3)	4.60
3.	Animal Husbandry	20 (23.5)	2.55	19 (12.0)	1.73
4.	Agricultural Programmes	13 (15.2)	1.17	7 (4.4)	0.62
	Total	**85**	**12.75**	**158**	**11.93**

Note : Figures in the parenthesis denote percentage of the number of beneficiaries benefited.

Source : Data collected from the Mandal Development Officer, Office of the Anantapur Rural Mandal, Anantapur.

It is observed from the Table—4.11 that the total number of beneficiaries accounts to 85 during the period 1996-97. In the year 1997-98 there were 158 beneficiaries respectively. The financial assistance given by the different financial institution is Rs. 12.75 lakhs in the year 1996-97, Rs. 11.93 lakhs in the year 1997-98. The number of beneficiaries during 1997-98 is less than that of the last year i.e., 1996-97. The total number of beneficiaries under ISB programme in two years works out to 120. The financial assistance given in two years for the rural poor under the agricultural programme works out to 6.43 lakhs. The number of beneficiaries benefited under animal husbandry is 39 members in the two years. The amount of loan component provided is 4.28 lakhs. The number of beneficiaries benefited under sericulture programme is 64 members in to two years. The amount of loan provided is 12.18 lakhs. Only 20 members benefited under agricultural programme in the two years. The financial assistance given in two years for the rural poor works out to 1.79 lakhs.

Out of this, top priority was given to the ISB programmes where an amount of Rs. 4.98 lakhs was provided to 103 beneficiaries (i.e., 65.1 per cent of the total). It is found that 29 beneficiaries (i.e., 18.3 per cent of the total) have received financial assistance to the tune of 1.17 lakhs under ISB programmes, 7 beneficiaries (i.e., 4.4 per cent of the total) have got financial assistance of Rs. 0.62 lakhs. It seems that less number of beneficiaries only 7 members (i.e., 4.4 per cent of the total) have received assistance to the tune of Rs. 0.62 lakhs. Though the number of beneficiaries received assistance is small still the financial assistance extended to them is greater compared to the agricultural programme.

Financial assistance provided under IRDP to attack rural poverty is being under implementation in two ways. Firstly, the financial institutions under the directions of the Government provide financial assistance in the form of loan and secondly, the financial assistance is being extended by the District Rural Development Agencies by means of subsidy. Component-wise financial assistance in the whole during 1996-97 to 1997-98 is clearly presented in the Table—4.12.

The loan component given by the financial institutions is Rs. 12.75 lakhs, Rs. 11.93 lakhs during 1996-97, 1997-98 respectively while the amount of subsidy given by the DRDA is Rs. 3.32 lakhs, Rs. 6.31 lakhs during the years 1996-97, 1997-98 respectively. The total amount of financial assistance (both loan and subsidy component) provided is Rs. 16.07 lakhs during the year 1996-97, Rs. 18.24 lakhs in the year 1997-98. So, the average financial assistance given per beneficiary is Rs. 18.90 lakhs in the year 1996-97 and Rs. 11.54 lakhs during the year 1997-98. The Table—4.12 shows that the moment of subsidy sanctioned by the DRDA is more in the year 1996-97 since the number of beneficiaries and the amount of loan are also more.

Table—4.12
Component-wise Financial Assistance
During 1996-97 to 1997-98

Sl. No.	*Item*	*1996-97*	*1997-98*
1.	No. of beneficiaries benefited	85	158
2.	Loan component (Rs. in lakhs)	12.75	11.93
3.	Subsidy amount (Rs. in lakhs)	3.32	6.31
4.	Total (Rs. in lakhs)	16.07	18.24
5.	Average assistance received per beneficiary (Rs. in lakhs)	18.90	11.54

Source : Computed from primary data.

Household Employment Levels of the Beneficiaries

One of the main aims of the financial assistance under IRDP is to provide gainful additional employment opportunities for the beneficiary household. The impact of IRDP on generating employment opportunities and the average mandays of additional employment's generated per household under each scheme is presented in the Table—4.13.

The table indicates that the mandays of employment among the beneficiary households has increased in all the schemes after the implementation of IRDP.

Table—4.13
Scheme-wise Employment Levels of the Beneficiaries

(in mandays)

Sl. No.	Scheme	No. of House-holds	Before IRDP			After IRDP			Total employment increase over pre-loan period	Per household employment increase over pre-loan period
			Male	Female	Total	Male	Female	Total		
1.	Industries, Service & Business	70	8632 (123)	3766 (54)	12398 (177)	11394 (163)	5837 (83)	17231 (246)	4833	69 (39)
2.	Animal Husbandry	20	1920 (96)	1420 (71)	3340 (167)	3424 (171)	1971 (99)	5395 (270)	2055	103 (62)
3.	Agriculture	6	540 (90)	450 (75)	990 (165)	1026 (171)	855 (133)	1881 (314)	891	148 (90)
4.	Sericulture	4	396 (99)	400 (100)	796 (199)	888 (222)	540 (135)	1420 (355)	624	156 (78)
	Total	**100**	**11488 (115)**	**6036 (60)**	**17524 (175)**	**16732 (167)**	**9203 (92)**	**25927 (259)**	**8403**	**84**

Note : Figures in the parenthesis denote percentage increase of income in the post-loan period over the pre-loan period.

Source : Computed from the primary data.

Irrespective of the scheme, on an average the mandays of employment per beneficiary family has increased from 175 mandays in the pre-loan to 259 mandays in the post-loan period, creating an additional employment of 84 mandays per beneficiary family. It is also interesting to note that additionally on an average 52 mandays of employment has generated to the males and 32 mandays of employment has generated to females in the post-loan period compared to the pre-loan period.

One of the five schemes the industries, service and business (ISB) schemes ranks first in employment generation for the beneficiaries. The total household employment of the beneficiaries under ISB scheme has increased from 177 mandays in the pre-loan period to 246 mandays in the post-loan period, indicating that the incremental employment of 69 mandays of employment per household over the pre-loan period. Under sericulture scheme, the total household employment of the beneficiary has increased from 199 mandays in the pre-loan period to 355 mandays in the post-loan period which indicates that the incremental employment per household over the pre-loan period works out to 156 mandays. Under the agriculture scheme, the total household employment of the beneficiaries has increased from 165 mandays in the pre-loan period to 314 mandays in the post-loan period indicating an incremental employment of 149 mandays per household over the pre-loan period. Under Animal husbandry scheme, the total household employment of the beneficiaries has increased from 167 mandays to 270 mandays from the pre-loan period to the post-loan period, indicating that the incremental employment of 103 per household over the pre-loan period.

Household Asset Distribution

The scheme-wise asset values of the beneficiaries and the average incremental value of the assets per household during the pre-loan period has been illustrated in the Table—4.14.

The table shows that the total asset value of all the sample beneficiaries assisted under all the IRDP schemes has increased

Table—4.14
Scheme-wise Distribution of Assets

Sl. No.	Scheme	No. of House-holds	Pre-Loan Period: Total Value of assets (in Rs.)	Pre-Loan Period: Average value per household (in Rs.)	Post-Loan Period: Total value of assets (in Rs.)	Post-Loan Period: Average value per household (in Rs.)	Average incremental Value of assets per household (in Rs.)
1.	Industries, Service & Business	70	2,09,184	2,988	3,55,612	5,080	2,092 (69.95)
2.	Animal Husbandry	20	1,86,300	9,315	3,08,382	5,419	3,896 (41.32)
3.	Agriculture	6	51,667	8,611	54,033	9,006	395 (4.58)
4.	Sericulture	4	92,000	23,000	1,81,240	45,310	22,310 (97.00)
	Total	**100**	**5,39,151**	**43,914**	**8,99,267**	**64,815**	**21,901 (49.87)**

Note : Figures in the parenthesis denote percentage increase of income in the post-loan period over the pre-loan period.

Source : Computed from the primary data.

from Rs. 5391.51 in the pre-loan period to Rs. 8,99,267 in the post-loan period. On the average the value of assets per household has increased from Rs. 43,914 in the pre-loan period to Rs. 64,815 in the post-loan period showing an increase of Rs. 27,861 lakhs.

The household asset value has increased to high level in sericulture scheme. Under sericulture scheme, the household asset value has increased from Rs. 23,000 in the pre-loan period to Rs. 45,310 in the post-loan period. Average incremental value of assets per household in the post-loan period over the pre-loan period is Rs. 11,270 (97 per cent). Next to ISB scheme. It had good impact on increasing the asset values of the beneficiary families. The total asset value of the beneficiaries under ISB scheme rose from Rs. 2,09,184 to Rs. 3,55,612 with the implementation of the IRDP. The average incremental value per household is Rs. 2092 (69.95 per cent) in the post-loan period over the pre-loan period. Under animal husbandry scheme, the household asset value has increased from Rs. 5,419 in the pre-loan period to Rs. 9,315 in the post-loan period. Average incremental value of assets per household in the post-loan period over pre-loan period is Rs. 3,896 (65.53 per cent). It had a good impact on increasing the asset value of the beneficiary families.

From the above analysis, it is clear that the average value of assets per household found to be highest under sericulture scheme at 97 per cent and the lowest under agriculture at only 4.58 per cent. The reason for the highest value of assets under sericulture scheme is that all the beneficiaries of sericulture scheme were small farmers and with the implementation of IRDP, they had very good chance to increase their productive asset base. From the foregoing analysis, it shows that the average asset value for all the beneficiaries under different schemes has increased after the implementation of IRDP significantly due to proper utilization of financial assistance provided under IRDP.

Household Income Distribution

The main aim of providing financial assistance under IRDP is to enable the beneficiaries to earn more income. So, that they may cross the poverty line. Hence, an attempt is made to present the impact of IRDP on income generation.

The scheme-wise income distribution of beneficiaries is shown in Table—4.15. The table clearly shows that the total as well as household income levels of the beneficiaries increased in the post-loan period over pre-loan period.

The total income of the beneficiaries rose from Rs. 6,99,380 in the pre-loan period to Rs. 8,71,993 in the post-loan period. The average income per household has increased from Rs. 7,255 to Rs. 9,12,525 after the implementation of IRDP, which indicates an incremental income of Rs. 1,866 in the post-loan period over the pre-loan period.

The scheme-wise analysis of the impact of income generation shows that the total income of the beneficiaries under sericulture scheme has increased from Rs. 37,600 in the pre-loan period to Rs. 49,619 in the post-loan period.

The average income of the household has increased from Rs. 9,400 to Rs. 12,419, which clearly shows that the average incremental income per household over the pre-loan period is Rs. 3,018 under sericulture scheme. The total income of the beneficiaries of animal husbandry scheme has increased from Rs. 1,26,000 in the pre-loan period to Rs. 1,76,400 in the post-loan period. The average income per household under the scheme has increased from Rs. 6,300 to Rs. 8,820 which shows that the average incremental income per household over the pre-loan period is Rs. 2,520. Under ISB scheme, the total income of the beneficiaries increased from Rs. 7,220 to Rs. 8,664 over the pre-loan period, which indicates that the average incremental income per household over the pre-loan period is Rs. 1,444 under ISB scheme.

The total income of the beneficiaries under the agriculture scheme, the total income has increased from Rs. 30,380 in the pre-loan period to Rs. 39,494 in the post-loan period. The average incremental income per household has increased from Rs. 6,100 to Rs. 6,582 which shows that the average incremental income per household is Rs. 482 under the agriculture scheme.

Table—4.15
Scheme-wise Distribution of Income

Sl. No.	Scheme	No. of House-holds	*Before IRDP* Total Income in (Rs.)	*Before IRDP* Average Income per household (in Rs.)	*After IRDP* Total Income (in Rs.)	*After IRDP* Average Income per household (in Rs.)	Average incremental income per household (in Rs.)
1.	ISB	70	5,05,400	7,220	6,06,480	8,664	1,444 (20)
2.	AH	20	1,26,000	6,300	1,76,400	8,820	2,520 (40)
3.	Agri.	5	30,380	6,100	39,494	6,582	482 (7.9)
4.	Seri.	4	37,600	9,400	49,619	12,419	3,018 (32.1)
		100	**6,99,380**	**7,255**	**8,71,993**	**9,12,525**	**1,886 (24.68)**

Note : Figures in the parenthesis denote percentage increase in income in the post-loan period over the pre-loan period.

Source : Computed frcm this primary data.

The Table—4.15 reveals that under all schemes, the average household income has increased from Rs. 7,255 in the pre-loan period to Rs. 9,12,525 in the post-loan period indicating an incremental income of Rs. 1,866 per household. The average household income works out to Rs. 7,255 in the pre-loan period. Since some of the beneficiaries have got more than Rs. 9,400. They got assistance due to local political interference and mis-representation of facts to the officials. The person who actually fall below the poverty line were denied the opportunity to get IRDP scheme to improve their economic conditions due to wrong selection of the beneficiaries. It should also be noted that an increase in income is only marginal since the incremental percentage in income is only Rs. 1,866 on an average per household. The incremental income per household over the pre-loan period is 32.1 per cent under sericulture scheme, 40 per cent under animal husbandry scheme, 20 per cent under ISB scheme and 7.9 per cent under agriculture scheme respectively.

The scheme-wise distribution of income is shown with the help of pie diagram in the figure. It is clear from the figure that the sericulture scheme has provided more income per household than the other schemes. The incremental income per household over the pre-loan period in 32.1 per cent under sericulture scheme, 40 per cent under animal husbandry, 20 per cent under ISB scheme and 7.9 per cent agriculture scheme respectively.

Summary and Conclusions

The two great problems of the contemporary world are (i) how the world community can avoid the kind of conflicts that might lead to nuclear war and (ii) how the world resources can be best utilised. So the mankind may be able to meet the urgent challenges of poverty and then more on the better things. The sad truth is that not much progress has been made on either of these fronts despite of the dialogue on disarmament and development. The ILO's Declaration that *"poverty anywhere is a dangerous to prosperity everywhere"*. Epitomises the importance attached to the challenge of poverty. The United Nations and its affiliates and initiating, either directly or indirectly several projects, schemes for poverty alleviation.

The literature on international poverty generated by the World Bank, FAOs, ILO and other agencies is quite extensive and diverse. The World Employment Programme (WEP) of ILO is well known and its basis needs strategy is evolved for poverty alleviation. The world bank's strategy was designed to improve the economic and social life of the rural poor by appropriate land reforms, agricultural credit programmes, education and health systems.

Among individual scholars, Gunnar Myrdal has made a significant contribution to the understanding of global poverty through his *"Asian Drama and The Challenges of World Poverty"*. The noble laureate Prof. Amartya Sen has also contributed in this direction.

In our country, particularly after independence, rural development is given a significant place in the five year plans. The growing inequality between the urban and rural population and between the rich and the poor in rural areas has brought the urgent need to develop these areas and the population thereof for providing the quality of life of the target group of families. Starting with the implementation of the community development programmes during early 1960s numerous attempts have been made and many programmes were designed and implemented during the Five Year Plans to develop the rural areas in general and weaker sections in particular. Today, rural development is considered as a process, aimed at improving the well being of weaker sections and has emerged as a strategy designed to improve the economic and social life of a specific group of people particularly the rural poor and the poorest among those who seek livelihood in the rural areas.

With the above objective in view, many development programmes were implemented with varying degree of success. But a review of the fact of these programmes reveals that the benefits flowed from these programmes did not percolate to the rural poor but were being taken away by the rural elite. Previously a mere project approach or a sectoral approach to rural development was followed which could only yield limited results. It was also observed that the programmes so far implemented were not adequate enough to lead to an overall development of a given area and proper distribution of benefits to the local population particularly the weaker sections of the area. Consequently, the attention of the Government has been concentrated on the integrated development of rural areas, the concept of integrated rural development with its accent on the scientific utilisation of all the resources available to create productivity employment opportunities and to generate income for the weaker sections in rural areas. So, that they may be lifted above the poverty line. In brief, IRDP aims at improving the socio-economic life of the poor and the rural weak in the overall spectrum of development and growth. It stress on increased production both in agriculture and allied sectors, emphasis on the role of village, cottage and tiny industries give primary importance to the tertiary sector to help the rural artisans and skilled workers in the rural areas.

The IRDP was introduced and extended on a large scale in 1978 to 1979 in 2300 blocks. In 1979-80, 3,000 more blocks were added to the programme. But from 2nd October, 1980, the programme has been extended to all the blocks of the country the 20 Point Programme. This programme is implemented at the district level by rural development agencies, in which priority would be given to Scheduled Castes and Scheduled Tribes in the provision of financial assistance. Even since the implementation of the programme, the total expenditure has increased significantly.

The main objective of the IRDP is to improve the income levels and to increase the opportunities of productive employment by strengthening the asset base of the beneficiary families. At attempt is made in the present micro study to analyse the impact of IRDP on income and employment of the beneficiaries. The study considers four sample villages in Anantapur Rural Mandal of Anantapur district. A total of 100 sample beneficiaries were randomly selected and interviewed, so as to collect the data on the impact of IRDP on their income, employment and asset positions.

The present study is divided into five chapters and a brief summary of the contents of the chapters are presented in the following pages The first chapter in the study deals with the introduction of IRDP. An attempt is also made in this chapter to review the performance of the IRDP at national and international level. Many evaluation studies on IRDP have been undertaken by different persons and institutions in different places of the country.

The second chapter presents the profile of the study district, research methodology adopted for the study and review of literature on IRDP. It gives a clear idea about the study district, research design, which contains the objectives, hypothesis, sampling techniques and the limitations of the study. Anantapur mandal was selected for the present study, which is socially and economically backward. At present the district has been divided into three revenue divisions. Anantapur division has 20 mandals and present study is made in Anantapur rural mandal. It is taken for the purpose of the case study to assess the impact of IRDP on income and employment generation. The sample villages were selected by following the stratified random sampling technique.

The third chapter deals with the background and the concept of IRDP programme. It contains with the objectives and the role played by IRDP at national, state and district levels. The administrative system of the programme at different levels is also discussed. But the special attention was paid for drawing the objectives of IRDP in particular which is a tool for rural poverty alleviation. The data presented in this chapter reveals its progress and achievement at different levels.

The socio-economic conditions of the beneficiaries are analysed in the chapter IV. These characteristics have been analysed under different heads viz., size of the family, age distribution, caste composition, literacy, operational holdings, income levels and occupational distribution. With the detailed discussion of all these characteristics, the study concludes that the beneficiaries have higher income and employment levels than the pre-loan period. Regarding the size of the family in all the target groups, the percentage of beneficiary families is high in the family size of 4-9 compared to the family size of 1-4. Age-wise distribution of beneficiaries shows that the working age group of people is greater at 67 per cent. The analysis of literacy and illiteracy levels of the beneficiaries shows that the total percentage of illiterates accounts to 23, which shows that the illiterates are less than the literates. The caste-wise composition of the sample respondents show that the 100 sample respondents, the Scheduled Caste households constitute 36 per cent which shows that a medium importance has been given to the Scheduled Caste families in the implementation of IRDP.

Scheme-wise beneficiaries, caste, income and employment levels have been analysed. The household assets, income and employment levels of the beneficiaries have been compared between the pre-loan period and post-loan period. The results of the comparative study shows that the beneficiaries have benefited much with implementation of IRDP. On an average, the value of assets per household has increased from Rs. 43,914 to 64,815 due to the implementation of the IRDP.

The analysis of income position of the beneficiaries indicates that the average income per household has increased from Rs. 7255 to Rs. 9121 after implementation of IRDP indicating on an average incremental income of Rs. 1866 household over the pre-loan period. The average income per household is greater than the poverty norm of Rs. 6400 due to the higher incomes of some of the beneficiaries. The persons who got income more than the poverty norm were selected due to the political interference and misrepresentation of facts to the officials. The people who really need support from the Government programmes were decided the opportunity due to the wrong selection of the beneficiaries. This type of selection should be avoided to benefit the genuine persons. On an average, the rate of incremental income per household is only 29.55 per cent. The average incremental value of income is highest in the case of sericulture scheme with 43 per cent over the pre-loan period followed by animal husbandry scheme (40 per cent), ISB scheme (20 per cent) and agriculture (7.9 per cent).

The analysis of scheme-wise employment levels presents the facts that the beneficiaries have better employment levels in the post-loan period compared to the pre-loan period. The total employment of the beneficiaries has increased from 175 person-days before the implementation of IRDP to 259 mandays after implementation of IRDP, creating an additional employment of 84 mandays per household on an average. Of all the five schemes, the agriculture scheme ranks first in generation of additional employment with the incremental rate of 90 per cent due to pre-loan period followed by sericulture scheme (78 per cent), animal husbandry scheme (62 per cent), and ISB scheme

(39 per cent). Repayment performance of the loan amount provided for the IRDP beneficiaries is in a deplorable condition.

Suggestions

On the basis of findings of the study, the following important suggestions are made, which may contribute to the effective working of integrated rural development programme.

It seems that the schemes under IRDP are utilised by the people who are above poverty line due to the wrong selection of the beneficiaries. It is necessary to take strong steps to identify the genuine beneficiaries without taking into consideration any political pressures or any type of bias.

The system of handing over the assets to some beneficiaries through the middlemen is not good in the interest of the beneficiaries, because they have to loose some amount by that way and they have no option to chose and purchase the assets with good quality. So the strict measures has to be taken by the Government to avoid this system.

There were quite a few cases wherein the beneficiaries do not receive the subsidy amount after the bank loan. Necessary measures should be taken to release the subsidy amount alongwith the bank loan.

The recovery performance is in a deplorable state. This is only due to the negligence as well as frequent transfers of bank officials. So the frequent transfers should be avoided and the Government should be given some guidelines to recover the loan amount within prescribed time.

The infrastructural facilities available for the implementation of the different schemes under IRDP are found to be quite inadequate.

There is no coordination and cooperation between the Government Agencies/Officials etc. Efforts should be made by the Government to bring cooperation and coordination among different agencies and officials to get good results of the different schemes of IRDP.

The insurance agencies should be very alert in releasing the insurance amount for those who have lost their assets.

Most of the beneficiaries were illiterate and therefore are ignorant about the IRDP and process of getting loans. So, adult education programmes, non-formal education programmes, and customer education programmes on bank schemes should be taken up by the DRDA or Block Development Officer/MDOs. With their primary knowledge and education they can get the loans without any difficulty or delay.

An inspection committee should be appointed on the beneficiaries, to check whether they are having assets or not. Those who are mis-utilising the assets should be punished severely and the necessary steps should be taken to recover the loan amount immediately by disposing their fixed assets.

The quality of the inputs supplied to the beneficiaries are reported to be unsatisfactory. Some amount should also be given for the beneficiaries to arrange a good shed for animals. This amount should be provided only to the beneficiaries of certain schemes like, bullocks and carts, sheep rearing, milch animals etc. The uniform pattern of assistance is also defective. Those villages which have been giving good response must be provided with additional funds while the villages giving poor response should be handled carefully.

The officials of different governmental agencies should extend their cooperation to the bank staff at the time of recovery of loans. This collective responsibility will be helpful for good recovery of loans.

There must be good cooperation and coordination between government agencies and banks on one hand, and the beneficiaries and these agencies on the other, which leads to the effective implementation of IRDP.

An effective implementation of this programme and the achievement of various objectives laid down for the programme can be thought of only with a whole-hearted involvement of all the agencies, departments and officials of the Centre and State

Governments, commercial banks, cooperative banks, regional rural banks, and officials as well as non-officials and voluntary organisations.

Finally, it is evident to say that the Integrated Rural Development Programme is one of the most promising programmes to change rural India. It is a great challenge to all the planners. Unless, they succeed in bringing about a drastic change in the way of life of the rural population, India can never join the line of the developed countries. IRDP will be implemented in a more effective manner in future to uplift the rural people in general and weaker sections in particular.

Bibliography

BOOKS

Abdul Aziz, *The Rural Poor—Problems and Prospects,* Ashish Publishing House, New Delhi, 1983.

Adams, Dale, *Undermining Rural Development with Cheap Credit, Boulder,* Westview Press, 1984.

Amarjit Singh and A Sandur, *Rural Economy in India,* Light and Life Publishers, New Delhi, 1982.

Arora, R.C. *Integrated Rural Development,* S. Chand and Company Ltd., New Delhi, 1979.

Azad, R.N. *Integrated Rural Development in Backward Area Development,* Sterling, 1982.

Aziz Saritij, *Rural Development Learning from China,* The Macmillan Press Ltd., London, 1979.

Bhattacharya, V.R. *The New Strategy of Development in India,* Metropolitan Book Company (Pvt.) Ltd., New Delhi, 1983.

Brown, Nathunial Banker, J. *The Role of Co-operatives in Alleviating Long-term Rural Poverty—A Case Study of Hancock Country Georgia,* Ph.D. Thesis, The University of Michigan, 1978.

Chambers, R. *Rapid Rural Development Appraisal Rational and Reporter,* Sussex, IDS, 1980, p. 20.

Dandekar, V.M. and Rath, Nilakantha, *Poverty in India,* Indian School of Political Economy, Poone, 1971.

Dantwala, M.C. *Poverty Then and Now 1870-1970,* Macmillan Company of India Ltd., Delhi, 1973.

Foneskar, A.J. *Challenges of Poverty in India,* Vikas Publishers, New Delhi, 1971.

Ghai Dharma, *Agrarian System and Rural Development,* The Macmillan Press Ltd., London, 1979.

Hanumantha Rayappa, P. and Deepak Grover, *Employment Planning for the Rural Poor, the Case of SC and ST,* Sterling Publishers (Pvt.) Ltd., New Delhi, 1980.

Kamble, N.D. *Poverty within Poverty,* Sterling Publishers Pvt. Ltd. New Delhi, 1979.

Khanna, B.S. *Participation of Non-Governmental Organisations (N.G.Os) in Integrated Rural Development,* Comilla, 1984, p. 159.

Khan, Wheeduddin and Tripati, R.N. *Plan for Integrated Rural Development in Pauri Garhwal,* National Institute of Community Development, Hyderabad, 1976.

Lakshman, T.K. and B.K. Narayan, *Rural Development in India—A Multi-Dimensional Analysis,* Himalaya, Publishing House, Bombay, 1984.

Madan, G.R. and Taramadan, *Village Development in India: A Sociological Approach,* Allied Publishers (Pvt.) Ltd. New Delhi, 1983.

Mehta Shiv, R. *Rural Development Policies and Programmes—A Sociological Perspective,* New Delhi, Sage Publications, 1984, XII, p. 192.

Minhas, B.S. *Planning and the Poor,* S. Chand and Company (Pvt.) Ltd., New Delhi, 1974.

Mishra, S.N. *Rural Development and Panchayati Raj,* Concept Publishing Company, New Delhi, 1981.

Morss, E.R. *Integrated Rural Development, Nine Critical Implementation Problems,* IRD Research Note No. 1, Washington D.C. Development Alternatives, Inc, 1981.

...kalatha, *The Poverty Issue in Indian Economic ... the 9th Century*, Ph.D. Thesis, Bombay, University ... 1978.

... *Rural Development with a Difference—A Monograph*, ... Development Cell, Manipur, 1984, pp. 2-3.

Gunner Myrdal, *The Challenge of World Poverty*: A World Anti-Poverty Programme in Outlines, New York, Paratheon, 1970.

Gunner Myrdal, *Asian Drama, An Inquiry into the Poverty of Nations, 3 Volumes*, New York, Pantheon, 1968.

Nagesh Kitle, *An Assessment of the Integrated Rural Development in Eastern Upper Voltra*, 1974-1981.

Omen, T.K. *Social Transformation in Rural India—Mobilisation and State Intervention*, Vikas Publishing House, New Delhi, 1984.

Ram Reddy, G. Haragopal, *Public Policy and Rural Poor in India*, Concept Publishing Company, 1985.

Rao, V.K.R.V. *Food, Nutrition and Poverty in India*, New Delhi: Vikas Publishing House (Pvt.) Ltd., 1982.

Rao, D. Vasudeva, *Facts of Rural Development in India*, New Delhi: Ashish Publishing House, 1985, p. 162.

Shampande, Yobert Kaneng, *Rural Development Planning and Resources Allocation Policy in Zambia*, Ph.D. Thesis, Columbia University, 1979.

Srivastava, U. and P.S. George, *Rural Development in Action*, Somayya Publications, Bombay, 1977.

Sundarama, T.R. *Rural Development for Weaker Sections*, The Indian Society of Agricultural Economics, Bombay, 1974.

Thekkanadai, S. S. *Rural Development and Social Change in India*, D.K. Publishers, Delhi, 1983.

The World Bank, *The Assault on World Poverty Problems of Rural Development, Education and Health*, The John Hopkins University Press, London, 1975.

Thimmaiah, G. *Inequality and Poverty: A Case Study of Karnataka,* Himalaya Publications House, Bombay, 1984.

Todara, Michale, P. *Economics for the Developing World,* Longman Group Ltd., London, 1977, p. 227.

Tripati, S. *Development for Rural Poor,* Revati Publications, Jaipur, 1987, pp. 41-42.

Vivekananda, M. and V.K.R.V. Rao, *Planning Unit Areas for Integrated Rural Development—An Exercise,* Ashish Publishing House, New Delhi, 1980.

Von Pischke, *Rural Financial Market in Developing Countries, Their Use and Abuse,* Baltimore, John Hopkins University Press, 1983.

Vyas, V.S. *Changes in Land Ownership Pattern, Structural Changes in Indian Agriculture,* pp. 181-183.

Weitz, R. *Integrated Rural Development the Rebout Approach,* Israel Settlements, Centre, 1979, p. 92.

JOURNALS

Ajay Kumar Singh, *Dedicated Administrative Support to IRDP—A Must,* Yojana, Vol. 29, No. 18, October 1-15, 1985, pp. 21-24.

Adhikari, C.S. *IRDP in U.P. Hills,* Kurukshetra, Vol. XXXI, No. 12, May 1983, pp. 13-16.

Anuradha, G. and B.P. Sinha, *Training under TRYSEM,* Kurukshetra, Vol. XXXIII, No. 12, September 1985, pp. 4-7.

Bharath Dogra, *Victims of Poverty Alleviation,* Economic and Political Weekly, Vol. XXI, No. 28, July 1986, p. 1193.

Bhadoria, P.B.S. *Rural Development: Problems and Prospects,* Kurukshetra, Vol. XXXIII, No. 12, September 1985, pp. 31-33.

Biswanath Ghosh, *Challenges of Poverty Removal,* Yojana, Vol. XXX, No. 18, October 1-15, 1986, pp. 4-6.

Chada Kavate, M.S. *Tardy Implementation of IRDP* Yojana, Vol. 29, No. 19, October 13-16, 1985, p. 13.

Chowdary, C.M. *IRDP: An Assessment of its Implementation*, Kurukshetra, Vol. XXXIII, No. 11, August 1985, pp. 15-16.

Correspondent, *Loopholes Infecting IRDP*, Yojana, Vol. XXIX, No. 18, Oct. 1-15, 1985, pp. 15-16.

Dandekar and Rath, *Poverty in India, Dimensions and Trends*, Economic and Political Weekly, Vol. XIX, No. 14, January 2, 1971, p. 40.

Editorial, *Khadi Gramodyog*, Vol. XXVIII, No. 1, October 1981, p. 5.

Editorial, *IRDP the Black Sports*, The Hindu, October 1, 1985, p. 8.

Editorial, *IRDP Reworking the Sums*, Economic and Political Weekly, May 25, 1985, pp. 898—899.

Gandhi, A.C. And R.P. Rawal, *Impact of Rural Development on Economic Status of Women*, Rural India, Vol. 49, No. 1-2, Jan-Feb. 1986, pp. 16-18.

Hag Mahaboob, Cl, *Employment and Income Distribution in the 1970's: A New Perspective*, Development Digest, October 1971, p. 7.

Jagadish Gandhi, P. *Peoples on the Poverty Line: An Overview*, Southern Economist, Vol. 25, No. 25, No. 17, Jan 1986, pp. 17-18.

Jose, A.M. *Peoples Participation and IRDP*, Kurukshetra, Vol. XXXIV, No. 11-12, August-September, 1986, pp. 41-43.

Krishna Bhaskar Rao, V. *IRDP to Alleviate Rural Poverty*, Kurukshetra, Vol. XXXIII, No. 11, August 1985, p. 18.

Krishnaswamy, O.R. *Strategy for IRDP*, Kurukshetra, Vol. XXXIII, No. 11, August 1985, p. 18.

Malyadri, P. *Success of IRDP—Myth or Reality: A Study*, Kurukshetra, Vol. 33, No. 11, August 1985, pp. 17-18.

Mohan Sundaram, V. *Rural Development and Poverty Alleviation: A Note on the Seventh Plan*, Southern Economist, Vol. 25, No. 12, May 1986, pp. 37-40.

Muralidaran, P.G. *Finance for IRDP*, Kurukshetra, Vol. 31, No. 3, Nov. 1982, p. 4.

Nageswar Rao, K. And M. Lakshminarasaiah, *Bank Finance and Rural Development in Andhra Pradesh*, Rural India, Vol. 48, No. 3, March 1985, pp. 42-46.

Nilakantha Ruth, *Garibi Hatao: Can IRDP do it*, Economic and Political Weekly, Vol. XX, No. 6, Feb 1985, pp. 238-246.

Prem Narain, *IRDP—A Critical Analysis*, Kurukshetra, Vol. XXXIV, No. 11-12, August-September, 1986, pp 8-11.

Raghunath Jha, *What Ails IRDP* Yojana, Vol. XXX, No. 16, Sept. 1-15, 1986, pp. 18-20.

Rajula Devi, A.K. *IRDP is Still the Best Bet*, Kurukshetra, Vol. 32, No. 3, December 1983, p. 6.

Rao, V.K.R.V. *Integrated Rural Development*, Southern Economist, Vol. 16, No. 14, November 1977, p. 9.

Rushendra Rao, CH. and B. Sambasiva Rao, *Essentials for the Success of IRDP* Kurukshetra, April 1985, Vol. XXXII, No. 11, p. 24.

Shantudu, D. *IRDP—Beneficiary Oriented Schemes: A Review*, Kurukshetra, Vol. 33, No. 12, September 1985, pp. 13-15.

Sivasubramanyam, *Rural Development, Programme in India: IRDP, NREP, DPAP and RLEGP*, National Institute of Rural Development, Hyderabad, February 20-24, 1984, p. 24.

Sudarsan, Gurajala, *Financing of IRDP*, Yojana, Vol. 29, No. 22, December 1-15, 1985, pp. 17-18.

Sudhakar Rao, B. *TRYSEM and ISB Components of IRDP*, Kurukshetra, Vol. 34, No. 8, May 1987, pp. 18-21.

Swarajpal Singh, *Survey on Socio-Economic Conditions and Awareness of IRDP*, Yojana, Vol. 28, No. 5, March 16-31, 1981, p. 24.

Thomas, A.M. *Meeting the Challenges*, Khadi Gramodyog, Vol. 28, No. 1, October 1981, p. 77.

Index